THE WOODBURY LINE

An Australian Convict Family

Ian J White

ISBN 978-0-646-86323-8

Published by the Author, in association with Ingram Spark, Melbourne.

First published June 2022

© 2022. Ian J. White

All rights reserved

No part of this book may be reproduced or transmitted in any form or by any means, graphic, electronic, or mechanical, including photocopying, without written permission from the publisher.

Review

It is no mean feat to research and write an interesting, entertaining account of a family line down through the years, yet Ian White, in his latest book, The Woodbury Line, has managed to do this—and, in my opinion, to do it very well. The Woodbury Line follows the life journeys of descendants of the Woodbury family from 1810 to the present and, by focussing on one branch in particular, Ian manages to bring their stories alive in a way that captured my interest and kept me wanting to find out more. Ian's clever weaving of fictional dialogue throughout his carefully researched facts about his ancestors also aided in this, as did his sharing of his own personal memories of various ones. There are periods of high drama in the book, as Ian recounts the involvement of family members in two world wars in particular, yet these are balanced well with more intimate moments and personal interactions that enabled me to appreciate the different personalities involved. All up, I found Ian's gentle, respectful style engaging and heart-warming—it is clear his desire in writing The Woodbury Line is to honour those who have gone before and to leave a loving legacy for those who follow.

Jo-Anne Berthelsen, writer and speaker
www.jo-anneberthelsen.com

This book is the second in the trilogy about my convict ancestors.

The first book in the trilogy is titled:

Elizabeth Rymes – A Remarkable Life

The third book in the trilogy is titled:

**Matthew James Everingham
Convict of the First Fleet.**

Details of all books can be found at
www.themustardseed.net.au/books

Ian J White

DEDICATION

For my two wonderful nieces, Krysten and Zoe, direct descendants of Sarah Elizabeth Everingham (known as Sally) through the Woodbury line.

Ian.

This book speaks in part about white settlement and the colonisation of Australia and affirms the dispossession of the original indigenous inhabitants.

The author acknowledges the unique status of Australia's First Peoples as the original peoples of this land and recognises their cultures, histories, ongoing relationships and obligations to the land.

About The Author

Ian has lived in parts of South-East Asia and in every mainland Australian state and territory.

For almost fifty years, Ian has worked in the foreign language industry, first serving twelve years in military intelligence, followed by twenty-five years teaching languages in Australian secondary schools and now, in semi-retirement, managing a small online foreign language translation agency.

Ian now lives in the beautiful Hunter Valley in New South Wales, not all that far distant from the areas in which Richard and Sally Woodbury née Everingham toiled and raised their family of 11 children. Ian now fills his days managing the online translation agency, gardening, reading and writing for his own pleasure.

Ian has authored more than twenty textbooks used in Australian secondary schools for the teaching of a foreign language and three books in the Christian non-fiction genre. He is also the author of *Elizabeth Rymes – A Remarkable Life* and, in many ways, *The Woodbury Line* is a sequel to that book, tracing the Woodbury line through the descendants of Sarah Elizabeth Woodbury (known as Sally), the eldest daughter of Elizabeth Rymes and Matthew James Everingham.

Details of all Ian's books can be found at www.themustardseed.net.au and readers can also contact Ian through that site.

Acknowledgements

Some people find that there are occasions in life when they are forced to take a pause, to look for a moment beyond themselves and to realise how many people have contributed to achievements that they, in moments of foolishness, thought they had achieved on their own. For me, this is one of those moments.

My cousin, Major Lynette Prince, recently retired from a lifetime of service as a Salvation Army officer, helped me with information about Salvation Army practices and history. Thank you, Lynette.

I am appreciative of the help provided by the Inverell District Family History Group, the Wing Hing Long Museum in Tingha, the Salvation Army Museum in Bexley North and Captain Henry Roehig of the Inverell Salvation Army Corps.

I particularly want to thank the research staff at the Glen Innes Historical Society for their invaluable assistance in searching the archives of the *Glen Innes Examiner* and finding the *Examiner's* report on the fall of Singapore in 1942. I am very appreciative.

In addition, I received invaluable help from members of two Facebook Groups:

Inverell and Surrounding Districts Memories
www.facebook.com/groups/1628177727444027

and

Convict Ancestry Australia
www.facebook.com/groups/940179979786378

Numerous people from both those Facebook Groups provided tips that helped point me in the right direction and I thank them all, with particular mention to Ms Robbie McLachlan, Marie Wharton, Rhonda Klenk and Sharyn Edmonds Cox.

Finally, I thank my editor, Jo-Anne Berthelsen. During the editing of this book, Jo-Anne's corrections and suggestions have made it a much better book than it was when I first passed it to her and there is no other editor I would prefer to work with. Thank you, Jo-Anne. You are a gem!

Ian J White
June 2022

Author's Note

The first thing that must be said about this book is that it is not going to satisfy the interests of all who are descended from Sarah Elizabeth Woodbury (known as Sally) and her husband Richard Woodbury. Sarah and Richard had eleven children:

- Richard Woodbury (II) (1811-1897), who married Jane Neal and had 12 children.
- Elizabeth Woodbury (1812-1876) who married William Hibbs and had 11 children.
- William Woodbury (1814-1886) who married Mary Ann Donovan and had 4 children.
- Jeremiah Woodbury (1816–1895) who married Mary Chaseling and had 8 children.
- Sarah Woodbury (1819-1904) who married Joseph Bridge and had 4 children.
- Rebecca Woodbury (1820-1887) who married William Craft and had 10 children.
- John Woodbury (1822–1883) who married Mary Ann Wells and had 4 children.
- Ann Woodbury (1824-1901) who married James Craft in 1840 and married again Adam Dovey in 1858. She was the mother of 7 children (all with James Craft).
- Jane Woodbury (1826-1897) who married John P. Cornwell and had 2 children
- Matthew James Woodbury (1828 -1835) who died at the age of 7.
- George James Woodbury (1831-1905), the youngest of Elizabeth and Richard Woodbury's children, who married Sarah Elizabeth Pate Charter, had 12 children.

Already we have a total of 85 different family lines, and we have traced only to the second generation of the Woodbury descendants. Clearly, the number of divergent family lines increases exponentially if one explores the next and subsequent generations.

I have therefore chosen to concentrate mostly, though not exclusively, on those who are in the same direct line of descent from Sarah and Richard Woodbury as I am, as shown in the very simplified diagram on p xii. I know that will disappoint some descendants, and I apologise, but there is a limit to how many branches of this family can be covered in one book without reducing it to a genealogical list of names and dates, and that has not been my intent. For those wishing to explore their family roots in other branches of the Woodbury family, I would direct you to Valerie Ross's excellent and exhaustive genealogy, *Cornstalks 1988 — A Genealogy*, Valross Pty Limited, Sydney 1987.

The other thing that must be said about this book is that large parts of it are fictional. The book is based, as far as possible, upon known facts about the Woodbury descendants but, of course, the daily dialogue and interactions between family members and with others were not recorded for us. As with my earlier work, *Elizabeth Rymes – A Remarkable Life*, I have therefore resorted to fictitious dialogue as a means of holding the story together. That fictitious dialogue, however, is often used as a vehicle for conveying factual matters relating to the family.

All dates and names of persons are as accurate as I have been able to make them, as are references to occupations, places of work, places lived and movements around various parts of the colony. If there are errors in the details of such content, then I apologise for flaws in my research.

There are places within the narrative relating to Australian political developments and, in those sections, readers might detect my republican sentiments. I know that I should have omitted those short sections but I felt they were relevant and important in describing the social and political evolutions of the times, particularly in the early decades of the 20th Century. Should any reader be offended by those sections, I apologise and can only plead my convict ancestry.

Newspapers and public speeches, where quoted, are quoted accurately and sources are cited.

Ian J White
June 2022

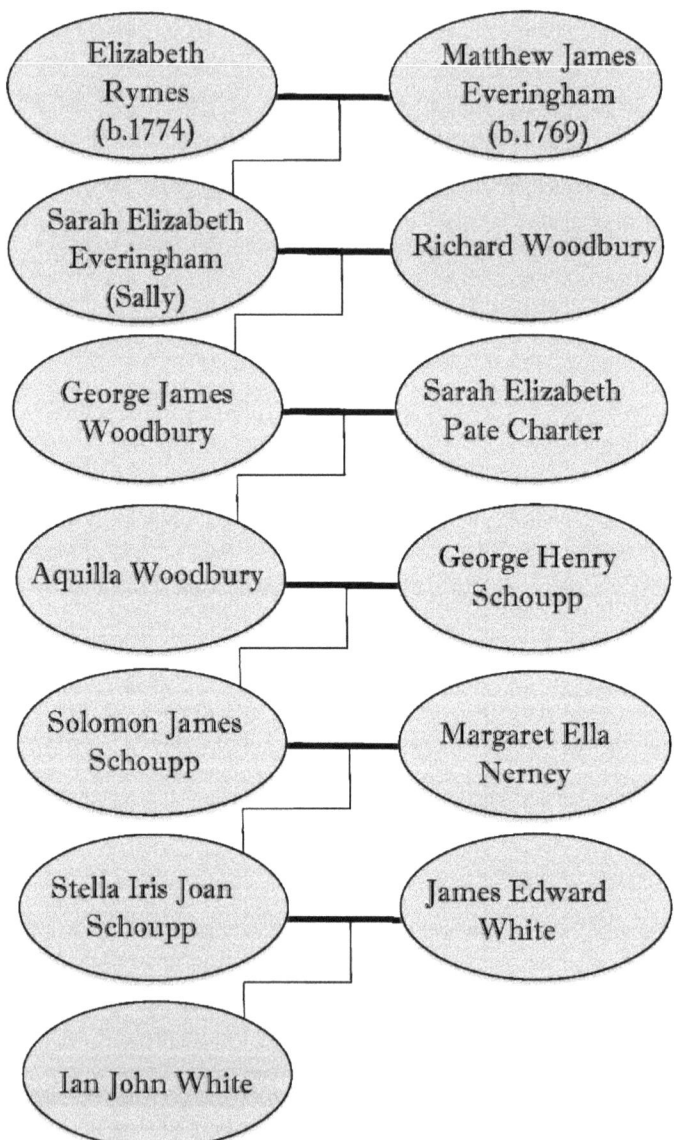

1

(1810)

"Waddya mean, y' said 'No'?"

Elizabeth Everingham née Rymes wearing her flour-covered apron and with her hands on her hips, stood confronting her husband Matthew James Everingham in the kitchen of the small, rented farmhouse. Both had arrived at Sydney Cove in chains, some twenty years earlier — Matthew on the convict transport *Scarborough* with the First Fleet and Elizabeth some two and a half years later on the convict transport *Neptune* with the Second Fleet. They had met at the Government Farm in Parramatta and were married there under a tree on the banks of the Parramatta River on 13th March 1791.

The ensuing years had been far from easy as they weathered floods, bushfires, and other natural disasters that at times brought them close to starvation and to financial ruin. Through all that, Elizabeth had steadfastly supported Matthew and the two had rarely, if ever, argued. In fact, she could not remember ever being angry with Matthew or disagreeing with him, but she could feel anger welling up within her now.

Three hours earlier, the local brewer, Richard Woodbury, had come in his Sunday-best to ask Matthew for the hand of their oldest child, sixteen-year-old Sarah Elizabeth, in marriage. Sarah whom they had always called Sally, had been born on 9th June 1793 at The Ponds, north-east of Parramatta, at a time when they had been struggling against the odds to eke out a living on their first land grant. Elizabeth loved all her seven children — Sally, born two years after their first child Mary's death; Matthew James Jnr born 1795; William born 1797; George born 1799; Anne born 1802; Elizabeth (II) born 1805 and baby James born 1807 – and had always tried not to have favourites, but there was no denying she had a very close bond with her oldest child. To her, Sally was special.

"Waddya mean, y' said 'No'?", she repeated when Matthew remained silent.

Matthew put on his hat and motioned with his eyes and a turn of his head that he wanted her to go outside with him, for this was not a conversation to be had within hearing of the children. Elizabeth followed him more than a little sullenly. He led her away from the house to a spot under a large eucalyptus tree where he had built a small wooden deck the previous year. During the early days of their relationship in Parramatta, they had often sat on a small deck built out into the Parramatta River as a landing place for the boats. It had been their special place where they had been able to spend time getting to know each other. Everywhere they had lived since that time — at The Ponds, at Sackville Reach, and now near Windsor — Matthew had tried to replicate that deck where the two of them could sit and chat. The deck at The Ponds had been destroyed by fire, and the one at Sackville Reach had been washed away by flood waters, but each time Matthew had dutifully rebuilt them. Their properties, of course, had not always bordered on a river, so the deck was not always a river landing place like the original one, but that did not matter. What was important to them was having that place where they could share happy times together. As they approached the deck this time, however, Elizabeth was more tense than happy, and she was sure Matthew felt that way too.

Matthew stepped up onto the small deck and then sat down, but Elizabeth remained standing.

"Sit down, Beth," he said. "Let's talk."

She sat down, facing him, and waited for him to speak.

"Have you seen the way some of the free-born settlers look at us? Have you heard their whispers? Have you heard the way they talk about our children as heathens and criminal spawn? Even in church you can catch them looking at us and talking like that."

Elizabeth sat silently looking at him. She had heard the whispers, she had seen women talking about her behind their hands, she had seen the looks of disdain.

"Richard Woodbury is an ex-convict," Matthew continued. "I want better than that for Sally."

"'nd what makes y' think that we's any betta than Richard Woodbury?" Elizabeth retorted. "You 'nd me is ex-convicts too, jist like 'im."

"Yes, we are," Matthew agreed. "We're no better than Richard. We're ex-convicts just like him. But Sally isn't! Don't you see, Beth? Sally is a free-born citizen of this colony. Indeed, she is the first free-born Everingham in this country. It'd be a huge step backward for her to be tied in marriage to an ex-convict."

Elizabeth closed her eyes, wanting for the moment to shut out this conversation. In their more than twenty years of marriage she had never, not once, had any reason to believe that Matthew held class-based prejudices. She knew even before they married that there were those who said Matthew was from a noble English family, perhaps even the son of an Earl. But Matthew had never talked about his family back in England and, until now, class differences had never even been considered, far less discussed.

"Do y' not think, Matthew, that Sally's 'appiness is important? 'tis important t' me 'nd it should be important t' you."

"Of course, Sally's happiness is important to me, Beth. It's been the most important issue in my deliberations," Matthew replied. "I've thought of little else."

"Well then, surely y' must see that what would make Sally 'appy is t' marry Richard Woodbury. That's what she wants t' do."

"Does she, Beth? Is that what Sally really wants to do, or is that what you want?"

Elizabeth recoiled in horror at that suggestion, almost as if she had been slapped in the face. This disagreement with her husband was starting to become a personal issue between the two of them rather than a discussion about the best interests of her daughter.

"Has Sally really thought it through for herself, Beth?" Matthew continued. "Does she realise that her children, like ours, will be subjected to discrimination and derision simply because her husband is an ex-convict?"

Elizabeth did not understand the meaning of "derision", but she didn't need to. The point of Matthew's reasoning had already been made clear to her.

"I'm surprised at y', Matthew," she said as she stood up. "Surprised 'nd maybe a little ashamed. I would neva 'ave thought y'd be one t' worry 'bout class differences."

Matthew opened his mouth to say something, but she cut him off.

"We'll talk more 'bout this, Matthew," she said. "Meantime, I think y' should stay away from Sally. She's gonna be really upset."

She turned and walked back to the house, tears in her eyes. Matthew stood and watched her go then kicked the deck in frustration.

Elizabeth went to look for her daughter Sally and found her in the kitchen, peeling vegetables for the evening meal, although it was clear her daughter's mind was not fully on the task at hand.

"Y've gotta remember, Sally, that y' father's a man," she said, as if that alone explained his obstinance. "Sometimes it takes 'em a while t' work out what's right 'nd what's wrong." She pulled Sally towards her, embraced her and kissed her on the forehead. "Y'll marry Richard Woodbury, Sally, if that's what y' want," she said. "It jist might take a day or two f' y' father t' come t' 'is senses."

Richard Woodbury had been born in Holcombe Rogus, England, probably in 1777 [1], to Jeremiah Woodbury and his wife Elizabeth. Richard had one older sibling, John, two older twin siblings Richard and Anne, both of whom had died in infancy, and four younger siblings: William, Anne, Jeremiah and Robert. It was not uncommon in that era for parents to give their children the names of earlier deceased siblings and of mothers, fathers, grandparents, etc.

Richard's mother, Elizabeth Woodbury, died in 1794 when Richard would have been about seventeen and, two years later, his father married Sarah Causey in Holcombe Rogus. Jeremiah and Sarah Woodbury would have seven children together, meaning that Richard's surviving siblings and half-siblings numbered twelve in all. Richard, however, did not know his half-siblings well, if at all, for by the time his father married Sarah Causey, Richard was working and living in Bristol. Indeed, some of the half-siblings were born during the time Richard was in prison in Bristol or incarcerated on the prison hulk *Laurel*, and Richard would be transported to New South Wales in chains before the birth of his two youngest half-siblings.

In Bristol, Richard lived in Current Lane, off Prince Street, and worked as a brewer in the employ of one George Taylor, a victualler on The Quay. On 30th July 1803, Richard Woodbury was committed to remand in Newgate Prison in Bristol[2] after being charged by George Taylor with having feloniously stolen six gallons of brandy to the value of £6, the property of the said George Taylor. Richard was convicted in the Bristol Court of Quarter Sessions on 24th October 1803 and sentenced to 7 years imprisonment with transportation to New South Wales.

He was returned to the Bristol's Newgate Prison and languished there until 4th August 1804 when he was transferred to the prison hulk *Laurel* in Portsmouth harbour, to await his transportation to New South Wales. Almost a year and a half later, he was transferred to the convict transport *Fortune* which sailed in company with the convict transport *Alexander* from Portsmouth, bound for New South Wales, on 28th January 1806, carrying a total of 306 male convicts. Richard arrived in Sydney Cove on 27th

July 1806. The census of persons within the Colony of NSW, held shortly after Richard's arrival, listed him as a convict labourer on the Government Farm at Castle Hill where grain crops were being cultivated to support the growing colony.[3]

Governor Philip Gidley King, the third Governor of the Colony of New South Wales, departed the colony within a month of Richard's arrival, to be replaced by Governor William Bligh. During his governorship, Governor King had encouraged the brewing of beer as a way of diversifying the economy of the colony and as an attempt to weaken the pervasive exploitation of the settlers by the Rum Corps. Early in 1806, King had provided a land grant to emancipist Andrew Thompson for the establishment of a brewery at South Creek, Green Hills, later to be known as Windsor. Thompson went to the Government Farm at Castle Hill in 1807 to select convict labourers to work his farm and his brewery in Green Hills, and Richard Woodbury, because of his background as a brewer in England, was a natural selection.

Richard worked as an assigned labourer in Andrew Thompson's brewery from about 1807 onwards and it was at Green Hills in 1809 that Richard Woodbury met Sarah (Sally) Elizabeth Everingham. In February 1810, because of his rapidly declining health, Thompson sold the brewery to ex-convict Henry Kable, and Richard found himself managing the Kable brewery.

This man then, one of the first brewers in the colony and one who was more successful and more affluent than Matthew Everingham himself, was the man Matthew had decided was not a good match for his eldest daughter.

There was still an air of unease when the Everingham family sat down together for their evening meal — mutton and vegetable stew with cornbread. As was their practice, the family bowed their heads whilst their mother gave thanks for the meal.

"We thank y' God, f' this food and f' all o' yer provisions t' us. We thank y' f' our family and we ask y' t' always remind us that all of yer children is equal in yer sight and that we's jist like everyone else. Amen."

As the family raised their heads, Matthew looked across the table at his wife.

"Do you think that was necessary?" he asked.

"Maybe we's in need of God t' be 'elping us t' keep t' our Christian values," Elizabeth replied. Then she dropped her eyes to her plate and kept her head lowered.

Usually there was a lot of conversation around the Everingham meal table but tonight, for quite some time, the family ate in absolute silence, all of them feeling the tension in the air. Eventually, Matthew pushed his meal aside and looked at his eldest daughter who raised her head to meet his gaze.

"Sally," he said, "I want you to know that when I spoke to Richard Woodbury this morning, what I said to him was said out of love for you. Nothing else, despite what your mother might think."

William failed to supress a giggle but was immediately silenced by a withering look from his father. Elizabeth continued to sit with her head down, her eyes focused only on her plate, but she was certainly listening and absorbing every word.

"I know that Pa," Sally replied.

Elizabeth sensed Sally wanted to add "but…", yet she did not. Instead, she continued to look at her father, knowing it would be impolite to plead her case.

"Your mother seems to think I was wrong. What do you think?"

Sally gasped, then held her breath. Indeed, it seemed to Elizabeth as if everybody around the table were holding their breath. She could easily guess at the thoughts rushing through her daughter's mind in that moment. Could she tell him what she really wanted to say? Was this an opening to plead her case? No, she couldn't do that. He was her father, after all, and she had been raised to always defer to him and to respect him.

"I'll do what you want, Pa," Sally said quietly in the end.

Matthew sat with his elbows on the table, his chin resting on his raised hands and intertwined fingers. For quite a few minutes he said nothing, and the silence became increasingly uncomfortable.

"Do you love him?" he finally asked.

At this, Elizabeth pushed her plate aside and lifted her head, casting a quick glance at Matthew. Then, with the slightest of smiles, she turned to look at her daughter and gave an almost imperceptible nod — more of a nod with her eyes rather than with her head.

It was obvious to Elizabeth that Sally was taken aback by her father's question. To talk to one's father about loving another man was something not only Sally but all young women in that era would have found intimidating, so she hesitated before answering.

"Sally, do you love him?" Matthew repeated.

"I do, Pa," she eventually said.

"And are you sure you really want to marry him?"

"I'm sure, Pa," she said, this time without hesitation. "I really do want to marry Richard Woodbury."

There was silence for several minutes before Matthew eventually spoke again, almost as if he had been agonising in his own mind about whether he should ask his next question.

"Have you thought through the issues, Sally? Have you considered the difficulties you and your children will face because you have an ex-convict as your husband?"

"I've thought about it, Pa. I've thought of little else. I was raised in this family, you know. I've seen the discrimination firsthand, yet, I still want to marry Richard Woodbury."

Matthew nodded slowly, looking first at his wife and then at his eldest daughter.

"Then you have my blessing, my fullest blessing. I hope you and Richard will be very happy for the rest of your lives, and we will do our best to give you a lovely wedding."

The audible sound of collectively suppressed breath being exhaled greeted Matthew's words, and Elizabeth smiled —

not one of those broad smiles that always caused her eyes to scrunch up, but a small smile of contentment. She winked at her daughter but said nothing. It would serve no good purpose to further undermine Matthew's dignity.

"Tomorrow morning, I'll go and visit Richard Woodbury and tell him he has our blessing," Matthew said.

1. There is some disagreement about the date of Richard Woodbury's birth. Descendants have placed a plaque on Richard and Sarah's grave in the cemetery at Wisemans Ferry in New South Wales, giving his year of birth as 1781 (see p.60). That date is disputed by the court records of the Bristol Court of Quarter Sessions which state that when Richard was tried and convicted before that court on 24th October 1803, his age was 26, which would lead to a birth year of 1777. The next year, 1804, Richard was incarcerated on the hulk *Laurel*, at Portsmouth, and his age was given as 27, confirming the 1777 year of birth. Later however, in NSW, Richard was listed in the 1828 census with an age of 47, which would suggest a birth year of 1781. Valerie Ross, in her extensive genealogy *Cornstalks 1988*, lists Richard's year of birth as 1781 (*Cornstalks 1988 – A Genealogy*, Valross Pty Limited, Sydney 1987, p.19) Today, descendants hold differing views about the true year of Richard's birth. What we can say, however, is that whether he was born in 1777 or 1781, he was significantly older than Sarah Elizabeth Everingham (Sally).
2. Not to be confused with the more infamous Newgate Prison in London.
3. 1806 General Muster of Convicts in the Colony (males). https://nla.gov.au/nla.obj-1280671362

2
(1810-1820)

Sally married Richard Woodbury at St Matthew's [Church of England] Church in Windsor on 17th December 1810, wearing a dress her mother had sewn for her, and a large straw bonnet. After the wedding, Sally and Richard moved into a small cottage attached to the back of the brewery at South Creek.

In the five years that Richard had been in New South Wales, he had done very well for himself. Having served his sentence, he was now fully emancipated, and his capital assets, including cash at hand, had gradually increased under the astute tutelage of Andrew Thompson. Apart from managing the brewery for Henry Kable, Richard was now dabbling in small-scale farming on leased land in the Windsor area. He was a tall man with a powerful physique, well suited to both farming and brewing pursuits.

In January 1811, just two months after their wedding, Sally informed Richard that she was pregnant. Richard was ecstatic.

"It'll be a boy," he declared confidently. "The first-born in the Woodbury lines is always a boy."

Sally smiled indulgently.

"Well, I'm not sure that's a reliable basis for a prediction. The first-born in the Everingham family was a girl, my sister Mary who died when she was only one month old. Then the next born was me, so I'm sure the

Everingham girls count for something in determining whether it's a boy or a girl. But boy or girl, I'll be very thankful for what God gives us. Mother and Father will be so pleased about this news. And Mother is pregnant too! What a sight the two of us will make in church!"

Sarah Elizabeth (Sally) Woodbury was known in Windsor as a devoutly Christian woman. Every Sunday, she and Richard attended the church service at St Matthew's church in Windsor, where they sat with her parents while all of Sally's younger siblings sat in the pew in front of them.

In early February 1811, the executors of the Thompson estate announced that an auction would be held to dispose of some goods and chattels formerly owned by Andrew Thompson.

"I think I should attend that auction, Sal," Richard told his wife. "There'll be items on sale that we can use to make our farming more profitable."

"I'll go with you, Richard, just to make sure that you don't over-spend" she replied with a smile reminiscent of her mother's broad smile.

A week later, the two of them attended the auction where they purchased a range of goods which they expected would be useful in their farming endeavours — twenty-five hundredweight of sulphur which in that era was used as fertilizer and insecticide on crops, together with casks, saddles, bridles, and a rifle. All told, they spent £17 3s. 6d.

"We should have bought some carpentry tools, Richard," Sally said on their way home from the auction. "There's something I want you to build for me."

"I'm no carpenter, Sal," he replied. "But if it's not too extravagant, I'm sure there are some building labourers around that could do the work for us. What is it you want?"

"You remember the small deck that Father built at the Thompson farm?"

Richard nodded.

"I want a deck like that," she said. "It's a family tradition."

"Well, I'm sure that's manageable. I'll make some enquiries around town and find someone who can do it."

When the labourers came to build the deck, Sally showed them her chosen place for it — a nicely shaded spot behind the cottage.

"Don't build it too big," she said. "No more than ten feet square and only six inches high. I want it to be smaller than my father's deck so he won't feel we've done better than him."

A new government initiative, launched in early 1811 by the recently arrived Governor Lachlan Macquarie, offered the loan of stock from government herds in an attempt to establish a private pastoral industry within the colony.

Richard made application to borrow a number of cows but suffered a severe accident in the brewery when a huge wooden rack holding a number of large barrels collapsed, breaking his leg and making it impossible for him to travel to Sydney. Although Richard was literate to a certain extent, he sought the help of his father-in-law, Matthew Everingham, in penning a letter to the Colonial Secretary. It was to Matthew that the whole family turned when such letters needed to be written.

By March 1811, Sally's parents and her siblings had moved into Andrew Thompson's Red House Farm in an attempt to diversify their sources of income. Because it was only a short move of two miles, Matthew decided to move the deck he had built at the smaller farm, rather than build a new one from scratch at the Red House Farm. He and his sons moved it in one piece to a site Elizabeth had chosen behind the Red House. It was there on this deck, that Matthew sat with his son-in-law and penned the letter to the Colonial Secretary.

Windsor, 3 June 1811

Sir,
In consequence of a very severe wound I met with in Mr Kable's brewery at Windsor I am at present prevented from attending His Excellency's order for receiving the Cows which are promised me and the enclosed certificate from James (illegible) Esquire [1] *will I hope be satisfactory on that score. Mr Kable who will be in Sydney is ready to sign the necessary Bond on my behalf and as soon as I am able will come to Sydney to undersign the same which circumstances, I hope Sir, you*

will have the goodness to represent to His Excellency the Governor whose Benevolence I trust will not let my accident deprive me of the indulgence.

I am, Sir
with all possible respect
your very obedient humble servant
Richard Woodbury

On 6th August 1811, Sally gained another sibling when her mother was delivered of another daughter whom she and Matthew named Maria Maud.

A little over six weeks later, on 21st September 1811, Sally presented them with the first-born of the Everingham second generation, a baby boy.

"Told you it'd be a boy," Richard said, beaming, as he held his newborn son.

"I suppose you have a name in mind for him?" Sally asked.

Richard looked at her incredulously. In his mind there was no doubt what his son would be called.

"His name's Richard Woodbury," he said proudly.

"Richard Woodbury Junior," Sally added. "It's a fine name."

Richard Woodbury Jnr was less than a month old when, after closing the brewery one night, Richard came home to the cottage and told Sally that there was something he wanted to discuss with her and that they had a decision to make.

"Sounds like we'd better go to the deck then," Sally said. "That's what it's for."

They sat on the deck enjoying the sunset and a pleasant cool breeze, as they sipped their evening glass of beer that Richard had brought from the brewery.

"It's good beer, isn't it?" Richard asked.

"Yes, it's nice. But is it the beer that we need to make a decision about?" she said, smiling.

"Well, yes, in a way," Richard said. "I've been offered the opportunity to buy into the brewery, to own it in partnership with Henry."

Sally pursed her lips.

"That's a big commitment," she said. "Can we afford it?"

"I think so. It might stretch our finances for a short while, but the brewery is profitable, the colony is thirsty, and around here in Windsor we have no competition."

Sally thought through the matter for a few minutes before finally responding.

"Well," she said, "I guess you know more about business matters than I do. I'll agree to whatever you decide, Richard, but thank you for asking me."

Richard sat silently, sipping his beer for a while, then nodded.

"I learned a great deal from Mr Thompson who owned the brewery before he sold it to Henry Kable. It's true I was a brewer before I arrived in this country, but he taught me a lot about business matters."

"He was a very good man, Mr Thompson. Mother and Father always speak well of him. They say he was always prepared to help the settlers. In fact, it was because of his kindness to our family that we came to live near Windsor after the disastrous flood at Sackville Reach."

"Yes, and he was also a very astute businessman. He built up large and diverse business interests, not only the brewery, but the fleet of Thompson trading boats, the saltworks, the general store, the tannery, and his extensive farms, of course. I'm sure I've left out some things."

"It's a shame he died so young," Sally said.

"Yes, but still, if he hadn't died when he did, we would not have had this opportunity now. Every cloud has a silver lining, I guess."

"And what do you think he'd say to you now, Richard?

"I think he'd say, as he often did say to me, 'Richard, you have to spend money to make money.'"

By the end of October 1811, Richard Woodbury and Henry Kable owned the brewery in partnership. To announce the business partnership, they placed a classified advertisement in the *Sydney Gazette & New South Wales Advertiser.*

> *MR Henry Kable and Mr. Richard Woodbury, beg leave to acquaint the Settlers on the Banks of the Hawkesbury, Richmond, and Nepean, and inhabitants in general, that they continue to carry on the Brewing Business on the same Terms as heretofore; and as it may be an accommodation to many of the former to be occasionally supplied with proportions of from Five to Twenty Gallons from time to time, on Credit till January next, K. and W. undertake to furnish such Quantities upon their Notes of Hand payable at that period. Any Commands will be punctually attended to.* [2]

In 1812, however, Henry Kable decided to concentrate on his other extensive business interests. He was heavily involved in farming, shipping, whaling, transport and retail and was ready to walk away from the brewing business. The brewery was operating in premises at South Creek, leased from the Andrew Thompson estate, and Kable came to an agreement with Richard Woodbury that he, Richard, would take over the full lease and fully own the brewing business.

The years from 1811 to 1815 were halcyon days for the young Woodbury family. The colony's economy was becoming more broadly based and was starting to emerge from the exploitative days of the Rum Corps' domination. The brewery was prosperous, and Richard continued to dabble in small-scale cropping in the surrounding area. In 1812, Richard purchased a house in George Street, Windsor, from the executors of the Thompson estate and rented out the house whilst he and his family continued to live in the cottage attached to the brewery building at South Creek. The couple's second child, a daughter whom they named Elizabeth after her grandmother, was born at South Creek on 3rd December 1812.

Just a few weeks after Elizabeth's birth, at the end of December 1812, the lease on the South Creek brewery site came up for renewal and Richard decided to purchase a site for the brewery in the heart of Windsor rather than renew the South Creek lease. He purchased a substantial property in Macquarie Street, Windsor, opposite the Windsor marketplace and moved his family and the brewing operations there. The George Street house continued to be rented out.

Sally was beginning to worry about the family's increasing debt and what she saw as Richard's cavalier approach towards such debt.

"These good times can't last forever, Richard," she told him. "We're starting to get into debt, and we need to be careful not to over-commit ourselves."

"One of the things Andrew Thompson taught me," Richard replied, "was to invest in property. 'Accumulate property,' he used to say, 'and you can't go wrong.'"

Sally was not convinced. She continued to worry about their debts, particularly because the Woodbury family was ever increasing in number, and her words that the good times could not last forever were eventually to prove prophetic. Meanwhile, their third child, a son, was born at the

Macquarie Street residence on 24th October 1814 and given the name William.

In February 1816, Richard advertised the residence and the brewery in Macquarie Street for auction and the property was sold in April that same year. After the sale of Macquarie Street, the family moved into the George Street residence. Richard had decided to quit the brewing business to concentrate on farming. In 1814, he had acquired two agricultural properties.

The sale of the Macquarie Street brewery proved to be providential timing because, in June 1816, the Hawkesbury flooded and large parts of Windsor, including Macquarie Street, were destroyed. The George Street residence was also impacted by the flood waters, but not to the extent experienced in Macquarie Street.

The first of Richard's agricultural property acquisitions was a 70-acre property at Cumberland Reach, about three miles upstream from Lower Portland in an area that would later be called Dargle. Richard purchased this property in 1814 in partnership with a John Bolton. The other property, bought at about the same time as the Cumberland Reach property, was an 80-acre property at Leets Vale, on the banks of the Hawkesbury about half-way between Lower Portland and Wisemans Ferry. Both properties were severely impacted by the 1816 Hawkesbury flooding.

Governor Lachlan Macquarie wrote, at the time of the Hawkesbury flood in June 1816:

> *"... a complete and awful Flood having taken place [in Windsor] ... to the great injury and distress of the Settlers residing on the banks of the river and creek, who*

will lose their houses and greatest part of the grain both in and out of the ground." [3]

Although Richard had been fortunate in selling the brewery property just before the flood, nonetheless the 1816 flooding of the Hawkesbury heralded a time of declining fortunes for the Woodbury family

On 28th June 1816, Richard was forced to sell the Cumberland Reach property at auction to clear debts and to meet the demands of his creditors. Sally's warnings that the good times could not last forever were coming true, but there were no recriminations — she would not say "I told you so!"

Times had also become more difficult for Sally's parents and siblings who had been renting the Red House Farm near Windsor from the estate of the late Andrew Thompson. They, too, had mounting debts and their situation was exacerbated when, in mid-1814, the executors of the Thompson estate put the Red House Farm up for sale. Matthew and Elizabeth and their seven unmarried children were forced to relocate to a small, rented farm at Portland Head. To some extent, they were fortunate that the Portland Head property was above the flood levels, but their two sons Matthew Jnr and William who were attempting to farm the family's property at Sackville Reach were far less fortunate and found their property periodically inundated.

Difficult times turned to absolute tragedy on Christmas Day 1817 when the entire extended Everingham family, including Sally, Richard and their children, were celebrating Christmas at the Portland head farm. Matthew, who had recently been appointed to the post of District Constable, was called out to investigate the claim that bootleggers were smuggling rum using a small sloop on the Hawkesbury. Only a few hours later, news came that Matthew had fallen from the boat and had been drowned in the treacherous eddies of the Hawkesbury. In later years, family members would claim there had been foul play, but the inquest at the time returned a finding of accidental death.

If such a tragedy had to happen, it was perhaps fortunate it happened on Christmas Day, when the entire Everingham family were gathered at the Portland Head farm celebrating Christmas with their parents.

"I hate to think how Mother would have coped with the news of Father's death if we had not been there," Sally said to Richard. "Can you imagine her getting that terrible news when she was alone?"

"She wouldn't have been quite alone," Richard replied. "Your younger brothers and sisters would have been there. But, yes, you're right. It was fortunate we were all there. You were a great comfort to her at that time."

"I worry about how she'll cope without Father," Sally said.

"Your mother is a strong woman. It'll be difficult for some time, but she'll get through it with the help of your brothers and sisters. We'll keep a close eye on her too."

Soon after the death of Sally's father, the Woodbury family left Windsor, renting out the George Street house, and moved onto the Leets Vale property. The move had been precipitated by the death of Sally's father because Sally had wanted to be closer to her mother. The property at Leets Vale was about five miles upriver from Wisemans Ferry and about the same distance downriver from the Portland Head property where Elizabeth Everingham continued to live with her younger children.

Life at Leets Vale could perhaps best be described as 'spartan' because a large quantity of household furniture from the Leets Vale property had also needed to be sold at auction, along with the Cumberland Reach property in June 1816, to satisfy the demands of their creditors. Sarah Ann Woodbury, Sally and Richard's fifth child was born at Leet's Vale on 3rd March 1819. Richard's efforts to farm the 80-acre property at Leets Vale, however, were frustrated by further periodic flooding of the Hawkesbury, particularly in 1819. The next year, in 1820, both the Leets Vale property and the George Street house in Windsor were seized by writ to meet outstanding debts. Richard, Sally and their five children were homeless and destitute, and Sally was pregnant with her sixth child.

1. *James (illegible) Esquire* was, presumably, a medical practitioner.
2. *The Sydney Gazette & New South Wales Advertiser*, Saturday 5 October 1811, p.4
3. *Journal of Lachlan Macquarie*, 1816. State Library of NSW, Manuscript Number, A773

General note
In the excerpts from *The Sydney Gazette & New South Wales Advertiser*, from the *Journal of Lachlan Macquarie* and from Richard's letter to the Colonial Secretary, it will be noticed that the text includes capitalisation which today's reader would consider unnecessary or wrong. However, these excerpts are reproduced exactly as they appeared in the original documents. The same will be true of subsequent excerpts from other newspapers in later chapters of this book.

3
(1820 - 1831)

With little choice, in early 1820, the Woodbury family moved to an extremely isolated land grant of 80 acres near Laughtondale. It was less than ten miles downriver from the Leets Vale property, but at the beginning of the 19th Century in New South Wales, it might as well have been at the end of the earth. There was no way to reach the Laughtondale property by road for the simple reason that there was no road. Their only way to contact civilisation was by boat on the treacherous Hawkesbury, with Windsor being the best part of an hour by boat in good conditions. They had no neighbours, the farm next to their property having been abandoned because of persistent attacks by hostile natives and escaped convicts. When Richard needed to go to Windsor by boat, Sally remained at Laughtondale, hoping she could protect her five children, if necessary, rather than expose them to the dangers of the river.

It was in May 1820 that Richard gained two separate appointments. The first was an unpaid appointment to the Portland Head branch of the Bible Committee which endeavoured to ensure that all families along the river had a copy of the Bible. It was a voluntary position and reflected the fact that Richard, as well as Sally, was a devout Christian. It was a role he took to with enthusiasm and fervour, notwithstanding the fact that it caused him to be absent from the family home in Laughtondale for extended periods.

The second appointment, at about the same time, was a professional and paid appointment as District Constable for the Lower Hawkesbury. Before applying for this appointment, Richard and Sally talked it over, sitting on the small deck behind their house near Laughtondale.

"It can be a dangerous job, Richard," Sally said. "I'll always remember how it took Father's life in 1817."

"Yes, I'm aware of that, Sal," Richard replied, "but it's also an important job. Someone has to stand up and maintain law and order in this country — in this district."

"But don't you think this area is becoming more law-abiding?" asked Sally.

Richard nodded.

"I do, Sal. And the role of District Constable hopefully will ensure that trend continues. But there will always be a need for law enforcement, even in places like Sydney, or London. Every society needs law enforcement."

"I suppose you're right," Sally said. "How much does it pay?"

"Ten pounds per year," Richard replied, "paid quarterly."

Sally rolled her eyes, a habit she had learned from her mother.

"They're generous, aren't they?" she said disparagingly.

Richard allowed himself a depreciative chuckle.

"Yes," he said. "It's not going to make us wealthy, but perhaps over time the salary will increase."

Richard submitted his application and was quickly accepted. Whether this was because there were no other applicants, because he had a reputation as a fair and honest man, or because he had a strong and imposing physique, they could not tell.

His beat as District Constable of the Lower Hawkesbury was extensive. It stretched from the confluence of the Macdonald River and the Hawkesbury, near Wisemans Ferry, all the way downstream to the area that would later be known as Brooklyn, not far short of the mouth of the Hawkesbury where it flowed into Broken Bay, a distance of about fifty miles. His salary as District Constable was not a lot of money for such a difficult and dangerous job which left his family alone and vulnerable most of the time.

As District Constable, Richard had two main responsibilities. The first concerned land which was granted to settlers with certain conditions attached. Settlers given these land grants were required to build a permanent house on the land and to display that they were using the land for cultivation. If these two conditions were not being met, the land grant could be revoked. Richard was thus required to visit the settlers to certify that the conditions were being met.

Although classed as an administrative task, this was not without dangers. Rebellious and unruly landholders could not be expected to give up their land without a fight just because they had planted no crops and, on occasions, the District Constable was met with violence. In most instances, however, Richard was able to persuade the land holders to comply.

"Look," he'd say, "you've got a house here. It might be a bit of a stretch to say that it's a 'permanent house', but I can exercise my discretion and say it is. The issue is cultivation of the land. I'll come back in a few weeks and if by then you've got a small plot planted with corn or maize, well, you'll have met the requirements. It doesn't need to be a large area of cultivation, just a small token plot will satisfy the requirements."

His second responsibility as District Constable was the maintenance of law and order from Wisemans Ferry to the end of his prescribed area near the mouth of the Hawkesbury. He was the arm of the law in a lawless part of the land and his role included the tracking and arrest of lawbreakers, hardened criminals, even murderers, escaped convicts, natives who had killed settlers, and any who did not respect the law of the colony. Think Wyatt Earp, without the handgun, without the horse, without his deputies, and perhaps without the wide brimmed hat – there you have Richard Woodbury, District Constable of the Lower Hawkesbury.

It soon became apparent, however, that Richard's frequent absence from Laughtondale made it all but impossible for him to cultivate his own property.

"I'll go to Windsor," he told Sally, "and apply for some convict labourers to work the land. Their presence here will also provide security for you and for the children when I'm away on my District Constable duties."

"Well, make sure they're good honest men, Richard," Sally said. "There are some convicts I wouldn't trust — some of them might actually be a threat to me and the children in your absence."

"I know the Commissioner of Labour in Windsor," Richard assured her. "We'll get good men."

A week later, three convict labourers were assigned to work on the Laughtondale farm — Patrick Russell and Robert Atkins, both serving life sentences, and Jacob Adler who was serving a fourteen-year sentence. The Commissioner of Labour had assured Richard that all three had been convicted of 'non-violent crimes and, to Sally's relief, all three turned out to be good, honest, reliable workers. Richard and Sally's sixth child was born at Laughtondale on 20th December 1820 and was given the name Rebecca.

In August 1822, nine convicts escaped from Port Macquarie, commandeered a whaleboat and loaded it with provisions stolen from a local farmhouse. They set out to sail south towards Sydney, believing they could blend in with the Sydney population. Near Broken Bay at the mouth of the Hawkesbury, however, they were caught in a wild storm. Their boat capsized, and all their provisions were lost. The nine convicts struggled ashore, starving and fortunate to be alive.

Settlers Adam Clink and his wife were less fortunate. The couple were beaten senseless with heavy clubs before the convicts made off with a new load of supplies from the Clink house. Word came to District Constable Richard

Woodbury the next morning and he prepared to leave in pursuit of the convicts.

"Richard," Sally said, "there are nine of them. You can't do this by yourself. You're going to need some help."

"Well, there is no help," Richard replied. "To get help I'd need to go to Windsor first. Then by the time I got some help and set out after these convicts they'd be long gone. I'm going to have to do this myself."

"You can't," Sally started, but Richard cut her off.

"Sal, I'll be all right. I promise you I'm not going to risk my life to bring these men in. If I can't manage it safely, I'll call off the hunt."

The convict gang had decided to split up and go their separate ways which, effectively, made Richard's task of arresting them easier. Capturing a united gang of nine would almost certainly have been impossible but by splitting up the convicts had strengthened Richard's hand. The leader of the gang was arrested within a mile of the Clink farm and taken to the Woodbury farm where he was trussed up and left guarded by a pregnant Sally, while District Constable Woodbury set off on foot in pursuit of the other eight members of the gang. Along the way, he enlisted the help of a neighbour, Thomas Walsh, and a young seventeen-year-old aboriginal man named William Gray. Together they apprehended all escapees. Richard secured the nine of them with rope, placed them in his boat and rowed them more than twenty miles to the holding cells at Wisemans Ferry. To capture nine desperate and hardened criminals was an outstanding achievement and reflected Richard's resolve to take his constabulary duties seriously. The Governor of NSW, Sir Thomas Makdougall Brisbane, commended Richard Woodbury, Thomas Walsh and William Gray for their efforts in apprehending a band of *"notorious runaways and pirates"* and approved a reward of sixty dollars,[1] to be divided amongst the three arresting officers.

Not long after this incident, on 5th November 1822, Sally gave birth to her seventh child, a son who was named John.

In his role as District Constable, Richard was a hard man who generally enforced the law to its fullest extent, but he was also a fair man, prepared to compromise at times when settlers were facing undue hardship and ready to stand up for those being unfairly treated or pursued by the law. One such incident occurred in June 1824 when Richard found himself being drawn into a dispute between a neighbour, one John Hunter who only days earlier had purchased the property neighbouring the Woodbury property, and Mr George Smith, the Provost Marshal's bailiff from Windsor.

Smith was attempting to execute a levy to recover debt on the property of a settler named Barton who had been the prior owner of the Hunter property.

"I'm not Barton," John Hunter shouted at the bailiff. "Me name's John Hunter 'nd I don't owe nobody nothin'."

"Doesn't matter," Smith persisted. "I'm here to execute this levy to recover debt on this land and that's what I'm going to do."

But in an effort to resolve the impasse, Smith and Hunter had gone to the Woodbury farm to seek out District Constable Woodbury.

"Well, actually, you're on my land. The land you came to execute the levy on is over there," Richard told the bailiff, as he pointed to the neighbouring property. "However, there's obviously been a misunderstanding. That's not Barton's land anymore. He sold it to John Hunter. You've no right to execute your levy against Hunter."

Smith still refused to desist, at which stage Hunter lost patience and punched the bailiff on the chin. A scuffle developed, during which Richard knocked down two of the bailiff's men and moved the bailiff off his property forcibly. John Hunter and Richard Woodbury were both charged with assault and released on bail of £50 each, with Richard paying Hunter's bail for him.

Shortly after being charged with the assault and bailed, floods again struck the Hawkesbury and washed away Richard's crops at Laughtondale. The flood, together with the fact that Richard was being paid a pittance for his duties as District Constable, found the family again in financial difficulties. The Laughtondale property had to be sold, and the Woodbury family, with their assigned convict workers, moved across the river and rented a property from Chief Constable John Howe in an area that was known as Gunderman. They would live there for the next four years, during which time Sally would give birth to three more children — Ann was born on 15th October 1824, Jane on 11th July 1826, and Matthew James on 15th July 1828.

Matthew James Woodbury would die at the age of only seven, on 25th November 1835.

In mid-October 1824, whilst Richard was still on bail for the assault charge, word spread throughout the Hawkesbury about a rogue aboriginal man who had left a trail of murder and assault from Newcastle to the Hawkesbury. In the Lower Hawkesbury the man had stolen food and clothing from a settler whom he viciously beat with a club and left for dead, although the man had survived and reported the attack to the authorities. Soon after, the aborigine had murdered another settler in the same area by decapitation. District Constable Richard Woodbury was instructed to investigate and, if possible, to apprehend the offender.

Setting out on foot, Richard made his way to Wiseman's Ferry where he asked the local aboriginal tribe whether they knew of one of their people who had attacked and killed white people. At first, he was met with sullen frowns and shaking heads but, after a few days of enquiries, he got a lead.

"Him bad fella," an old aboriginal man said to him. "Good you stay away from him."

"So, you know him!" Richard said. "What's his name?"

"Him name Devil-Devil," the old man said. "Him wild fella," he added, using his finger to draw small circles on his head.

A crazy man, perhaps even totally insane, Richard thought, whilst nodding to the old aboriginal man.

"Will you help me find him?"

The old man shook his head. Richard realised then that this old man and probably most of the tribe were clearly afraid of Devil-Devil. But before the old man turned his back and walked away, he pointed north.

The next day, Richard set out north by foot through the bush, searching for signs of Devil-Devil. He came across other aboriginal people but, when he mentioned the name Devil-Devil to them, they were clearly afraid. In response to Richard's requests for assistance, they simply pointed north. For more than ten days, Richard tracked Devil-Devil through the Australian bush, occasionally coming across the remains of small fires and packaging from food that had clearly been stolen from settlers. On the twelfth day, he came across a wild looking aboriginal man with matted hair camped by a small waterhole. District Constable Richard Woodbury had found his man and, because of his sheer size and strength, he was able to apprehend Devil-Devil. He tied the man's hands behind his back, looped a rope around his neck and led him to the gaol at Wisemans Ferry where he was charged with murder. For a white man to track and arrest a murderous aboriginal man in the Australian bush environment was an extraordinary feat.

The *Sydney Gazette & New South Wales Advertiser* reported on the indictment of Devil-Devil on 11th November 1824.

> *On Saturday, the 30th ult. Devil-Devil, an able-bodied aboriginal native, with a cloven foot, was brought before a Bench of Magistrates at Windsor by Woodbury, a Portland-Head constable, charged with murdering a servant of Mr Dickson's in the bush, by severing the*

> *poor man's head from his body with a tomahawk, while in the act of stooping down to the ground. The sable criminal was remanded for further examination.*[3]

"Not a very extensive report," Sally said as she sat at the dinner table reading the Gazette. "It gives no details of the difficulties you faced in tracking him down, nor really of how evil the man is."

Richard nodded and looked at his wife over the rim of his pannikin of tea.

"Hmm, well I'm happy keeping a low profile. And I suspect the authorities aren't saying much about Devil-Devil until they have determined whether he's of sound mind. He may be totally unhinged — perhaps not even responsible for his criminal actions."

It was soon after the apprehending of Devil-Devil that the charge against Richard Woodbury and his neighbour, John Hunter, of assaulting the bailiff and his men came before the court. The *Sydney Gazette & New South Wales Advertiser* reported on the court proceedings on 2nd December 1824.

> *Richard Woodbury and John Hunter, charged with committing an assault in June last, on Mr George Smith, Provost Marshal's Bailiff, in the execution of his duty. The charge was not substantiated. It appeared in evidence that Smith had to levy an execution on the property of one Barton, near the lower branch of the Hawkesbury River. The property consisting of a farm with the growing crop, was sold to Hunter a few days before the writ was issued. Of this fact, Smith was*

appraised by both parties; but he still insisted on executing the writ, on which Hunter called on Woodbury, who is the District Constable, to defend his property. It appeared too, that Smith had mistaken the farm that had belonged to Barton and was actually at Woodbury's ground when he attempted to make the levy. Here the scuffle occurred, in which Woodbury pushed the Bailiff [out] *of his wheat into the path. The Chairman observed that there did not appear to him to be any ground for the indictment, as Smith was seizing on the property not of Barton but on another person, and that no unnecessary violence was used in repelling the invasion. The prisoners were acquitted.*[2]

In England, the predominant Christian denomination was the Church of England, of which the reigning monarch was, and is, the titular head. Richard and Sally Woodbury were devout Christians who raised their children within the catechism of the Church of England. But, in the early part of the 19th Century the Christian religion in New South Wales was diversifying, particularly amongst those who saw the Church of England as being the church of the ruling class.

Reverend Samuel Leigh, a Wesleyan minister, arrived in Sydney on board the *Herbe* on 10th August 1815. At first, he was given little encouragement and a less than warm welcome by Governor Lachlan Macquarie who wrote to British government stating that, despite the Reverend's exemplary conduct, in future the colony would appreciate only ministers of the Church of England faith.

With his obvious sincerity and commitment to the Christian church, however, Leigh eventually won the admiration of Macquarie. He established churches in Sydney and preaching places in Parramatta, Liverpool, Castlereagh on the Nepean River and Windsor on the Hawkesbury. Leigh established the first Wesleyan circuit in New South Wales and, by the 1820s, groups of Methodists were active in many parts of the colony, including along the Hawkesbury.

While living in the Gunderman area, Richard and Sally Woodbury gravitated towards Wesleyan Methodism which they saw as a revivalist and secessionist alternative to the Church of England. The Woodbury children born in 1826 and 1828, Jane and Matthew, were baptised according to the rites of the Wesleyan Church, and the Woodbury home at Gunderman became a regular venue in the Wesleyan preaching circuit of the Hawkesbury. Caroline Love née Woodbury, the daughter of George James Woodbury and granddaughter of Richard and Sally Woodbury, later recorded that:

> *"Grandfather and Grandmother opened their house to religious service for as long as I can remember, and the Wesleyan local preachers used to have services there every Sunday ... people came for miles in boats to be at the services"*[4]

Much later, in 1855, the Lower Hawkesbury Wesleyan Chapel, which still stands, was built on land that had been the Woodbury farm at Gunderman. Over time, some of the growing Woodbury family and subsequent generations, would embrace yet other Christian denominations.

The property at Gunderman, including the house and all belongings of the Woodbury family, was destroyed by fire on 23rd January 1827, leaving the Woodbury family destitute, with nothing other than the clothes they stood in. The fire was a dreadful accident which occurred when the son of a neighbouring family, one referred to as "young Green", set fire to corn stubble on the Green family property. *The Sydney Gazette & New South Wales Advertiser* reported the incident in detail and also noted the esteem in which Richard Woodbury was held within the Hawkesbury community.

> *We have to record a disaster which may be truly called, a dreadful conflagration, the effects of which will most undoubtedly sink a large family into extreme distress. On Wednesday, the 23rd instant, young Green (using the familiar term applied in the communication made to us) set fire to his stubble. When he commenced this job, the weather was well suited to the undertaking, but a gust of wind suddenly arose, and drove the fire before it with dreadful rapidity; an alarm was soon spread, but all exertion to extinguish the flames proved fruitless. The fire spread across the bottom of a marsh, dried by the droughty season, the grass burning in all directions for more than a mile in circumference; at length it reached three corn houses on the farm of Richard Woodbury, district constable of the lower branch, which, alike exceedingly dry, burnt with a quickness most dreadful and astonishing, and very soon reduced the whole to cinders. The corn houses were at least fifteen or sixteen yards off the dwelling, and to give the reader some idea of the spreading flames, we mention that although there*

was no rubbish or dry grass before the door, the whole caught fire, defying all efforts to extinguish it. The unfortunate family of nine children, were scarcely left with clothes sufficient to cover them. Mr Woodbury has been several years a district constable and is more esteemed than many persons holding similar situation in life. The fire so encircled the premises that all the poultry were destroyed, not being able to fly over it. The pigs are the only property saved.[5]

Within a year, however, Richard and his family had rebuilt the home and the farm at Gunderman. The Gunderman farm had a total of seventy acres, sixty of which were under cultivation. In addition, the family was grazing small herd of cattle. The Woodburys also employed John Harman who had married Sally's younger sister Elizabeth Butler née Everingham in 1827 and the Harman family also resided on the Gunderman farm. In addition, Richard Woodbury had a number of assigned convict workers — three labourers, a stonemason, a blacksmith and a female house servant. The specific assignment of a stonemason and a blacksmith were indicative of Richard's desire to diversify his commercial interests.

A group of four convicts, Richard Payne, Thomas Bagley, Patrick Dayley and John Rothwell, absconded during the afternoon of 4th October 1828 from the Number Three Iron Gang which was working on the construction of the Great North Road being built to link Sydney with the fertile Hunter Valley to the north. As they travelled through the bushland of the Lower Hawkesbury, the escapees armed themselves with heavy sticks which they believed could be used as clubs either to defend themselves against recapture or to attack any unwary settlers they might come across. Richard Payne was the leader of the group and swore murderous threats as the group made their way through the bush.

"By God," Payne said, "I'll have something tonight or I'll have someone's head."

John Rothwell would later testify that such threats by Payne disturbed him as he himself wanted no part in any violence.

The escapees were approaching the Woodbury house on the night of 4th October when, by chance, Richard had come outside the house because the dogs were barking. Seeing the men nearby and not suspecting that they were convict escapees, Richard called the dogs off.

"Who are you?" he asked them.

"And b' Jesus who are you?" Payne shouted in reply, as he attempted to land a blow on Richard's head with the club he was carrying. Fortunately, Richard warded off the blow with his arm and quickly retreated into the house, followed by Payne, Bagley and Dayley. Rothwell, still not wanting any part in violence, remained outside, and the labourers assigned to the Woodbury property fled — some in fear and others in search of assistance.

Inside the house, Sally and two children were forced to lie in a corner of the room, guarded by Dayley, while the other two set about beating Richard senseless with their clubs. Looking about for a weapon with which to defend himself, Richard took hold of a glass bottle and attempted to strike one of the assailants with it but was thwarted in that effort when Bagley wrested the bottle from him and struck

Richard violently over the head with it. A fire was burning in the hearth and Payne was making every effort to push Richard into it and set him alight. The three assailants were clearly intent on taking Richard's life, then perhaps, having their way with Sally.

The sound of a shotgun blast in the small house was deafening and stunned everyone in the room, none more so than Payne who had taken some of the shot in his neck. Richard's young son, William, stood in the doorway to the bedroom with his father's smoking gun in his hands. In a matter of three seconds, while the three assailants were still stunned, he quickly broke the gun and inserted a new cartridge, snapping the gun back into position and pulling back the hammer, ready to fire another shot.

Bagley and Dayley quickly assisted Payne and the three assailants fled the house. Two days later, John Rothwell surrendered himself to police and the other three escapees were soon apprehended.

Richard had been severely beaten in the attack. He had numerous broken bones and many fragments of glass were removed from his head. These were serious injuries in a time when medical assistance, even if available, was rudimentary. Following the attack, he was confined to bed for some weeks, where Sally read the report from the *Sydney Gazette & New South Wales Advertiser* to him as she sat on the edge of his bed

> *A desperate attack was made, a fortnight ago, on the house of Richard Woodbury, district constable of the Lower Branch, by four men, armed with formidable bludgeons. Without ceremony, they began to beat him in the most furious manner and would doubtless very soon*

have deprived him of life, had it not been for the heroic conduct of his little son. The boy seeing his father's danger, slily [sic] *entered the bedroom, took down a gun loaded with slugs, and though it was almost beyond his strength even to lift it, the little fellow contrived to discharge its contents into the neck of one of the villains. They immediately decamped, carrying with them, their wounded accomplice. One of the gang members was apprehended two days after, and confessed the whole truth, in consequence of which, the other three have been since lodged in custody.*[6]

"This report makes is appear as if William is a toddler," Sally said with a smile. "It describes him as our 'little son' and says that the gun was so heavy that it 'was almost beyond his strength even to lift it'. Don't they know William is fourteen years old?"

Richard, still recovering from the attack, chuckled at Sally's words, then grimaced in pain and reached to hold his broken ribs.

"I guess they think that portraying William as younger than he really is makes a good story," he said. "One thing is for sure, I'm certainly glad he was able to lift that gun and fire it."

One day during his recuperation, after he started to move about the house on roughly made crutches, he went in search of Sally and found her sitting on the deck at the rear of the house — their place of meeting

"I suppose this means there's something you want to talk about?" he asked, as he sat down on the deck with her. Sally smiled and sipped from her pannikin of tea but said nothing for some time.

"How are you feeling?" she eventually asked.

"I'll mend," Richard replied. "Still sore, but I'll mend."

"Richard," Sally said, "I want you to resign from the post of District Constable."

"Go on," he replied as he looked at her.

"It's a dangerous job, and for what? £10 a year? We'd be better off, and safer, if we concentrated on farming."

Richard nodded and thought about the matter for a few minutes.

"I don't do it for the money. I do it because it's an important job. This is a harsh country, Sal, filled with convicts and ex-convicts, many of whom retain their inclination for crime and violence. Without law enforcement, this country would quickly become wild and ungovernable."

There were a few moments of silence before Richard continued.

"And that attack on our family last month had nothing to do with my job as District Constable," he said. "They didn't even know whose house it was."

"Still, I worry constantly about you," Sally said. "And I worry about us. Being a District Constable cost my father his life."

Richard nodded but said nothing.

"I don't know how the children and I would cope if something happened to you," Sally continued.

"Okay," Richard said, nodding in agreement.

"And what's more," Sally began, only to stop as she realised what Richard had said. "Okay? You mean, 'Okay, I'll resign', just like that?"

She could hardly believe Richard had actually agreed to her suggestion.

"Yes, okay!" Richard said then with a smile. "It's something I've been thinking about too. As I said, it's an important job, it has to be done, but it doesn't have to be done by me. Anyway, I've done it for near on nine years now. It's time they found a good man to replace me."

Richard was eventually replaced by two District Constables to cover the same area that he had covered by himself.

Despite the fire and the attack on their home at Gunderman, Richard and Sally had been able to achieve a certain level of affluence, at least enough to be able to live comfortably. They were given a land grant of fifty acres down-river at Mangrove Creek, whereupon they bought the property at Gunderman then quickly on-sold it at a modest profit. Immediately after the sale of the Gunderman property Richard moved his family to the Mangrove Creek property where, for a short period in 1830, he was contracted to the Commissary Department for the supply of food provisions to the number nine Iron Gang working on the Great North Road. Things were going so well that Richard asked himself why he had not quit the position of District Constable much earlier than he had.

In 1830, the family moved a short distance to a seventy-acre farm at Popran Creek. Soon after, Richard bought another thirty-acre property opposite Sugee Bag Creek, about five miles further upstream, and the family moved again. It was here that Richard and Sally's daughter, Elizabeth, met a neighbouring landholder's son, William Hibbs.

On 26th January 1788, Peter Hibbs had arrived in the colony as a free man, a sailor on *Sirius,* as part of the First Fleet. He was sent to Norfolk Island in 1790 and there he married Mary Pardoe, a convict who had arrived on the convict ship *Lady Juliana.* Together, they had four sons, of whom William Hibbs was the third son, born on 6th January 1804. By the mid-1820s, Peter Hibbs, his wife Mary Hibbs and their four sons were living in the Portland Head area of the Hawkesbury.

William Hibbs and Elizabeth Woodbury were married at Sackville Reach on 19th January 1830 and the couple, through their ten children, would establish another extensive branch of Woodbury descendants, albeit bearing the Hibbs name, mostly in the districts of Mangrove Creek,

Brisbane Waters, Gosford and Wollombi in the Hunter valley.

Indeed, the move of Richard and Sally's family to the Mangrove Creek area in 1830 would make the Mangrove Creek district the jumping-off point for the migration of later members of the Woodbury family through Mangrove to Wollombi, Millfield, Brisbane Waters, Gosford and further up the Hunter Valley. At the time of the family's move to Sugee Bag Creek, Richard Woodbury was fifty-four years of age and Sally thirty-eight. Over the course of the previous twenty years, Sally had given birth to ten children and she wasn't finished yet.

In 1828, Richard had made application to rent 100 acres of land at Mangrove Creek — land which had been set aside for future use by the church. His application, whilst not being outright refused, was stalled in negotiations between the church and the Lands Grant office in Sydney. Those negotiations had gone on for almost two years.

"Have you heard anything about our application to rent the church land?" Sally asked her husband one day.

"No. I don't understand what's holding up our application, Sal," Richard replied. "They've been mulling over it for so long. Surely the government and the church can both see that we are well established farmers in this area and that we can make profitable use of the land."

"My father always said the government can't make quick decisions," Sally replied. "Maybe we should get some high ranking official from within the church to support our application."

Richard sipped his tea and nodded while he thought about that idea.

"I'll talk to the pastor next time he's here," he said.

It was some two months later when, on the pastor's advice, Richard enlisted the aid of the Church of England catechist, James Chandler, in resubmitting his application to lease the church reserve land.

> *Richard Woodbury,* Chandler wrote, *has served for many years as representative of the Portland Head Branch of the Bible Committee. He and his wife, support a family of nine children, all of whom are devout Christian souls, and they open their home for services conducted by preachers from the Wesleyan Methodist preaching circuit. Richard Woodbury also served with distinction as a District Constable for almost ten years and I therefore consider him to be a more than appropriate person to be granted a lease on church land.*

Richard, for his part, wrote that he had a small herd of cattle and £600 in hand as security for the lease.

Finally, this resubmission was successful and Richard was granted a grazing lease on the church reserve land.

1. The Colonial Government of NSW in those times often made reference to payment in "dollars". At that time there was little NSW coinage and the term "dollars" referred to Spanish pieces of eight (Spanish silver dollars cut into eight segments) which were recognised and distributed by the government, and valued on a set exchange rate relative to English pounds
2. *Sydney Gazette & New South Wales Advertiser*, 2 December 1824, p.3. Word in brackets added by the author.
3. *Sydney Gazette & New South Wales Advertiser,* 11 November 1824, p.2.
4. Ross, V. *A Hawkesbury Story.* Valross Pty Limited, Sydney, 1981, (Library of Australian History)
5. *Sydney Gazette & New South Wales Advertiser*, 31 January 1827, p.2.
6. *Sydney Gazette & New South Wales Advertiser*, 31 October 1828, p.2.

4
(1831 – 1874)

Richard and Sally's last child was born at Mangrove Creek on 19th December 1831 – a healthy and strong baby boy to whom they gave the name George James.

Meanwhile, the older Woodbury children were seeking out marriage partners and the grandchildren of Richard and Sally were coming thick and fast. Those grandchildren would go on to establish extensive branches of the Woodbury line and make the Woodbury name well known and influential amongst the settlers of Mangrove Creek and the Lower Hawkesbury districts.

Sarah Woodbury, known as Annie, married Joseph Bridge at the Lower Hawkesbury on 28th April 1834. They would have four children in an unhappy marriage caused by Joseph's frequent and extended absences from the family home before he finally abandoned Sarah entirely.

Richard and Sally's third child, William, married Mary Ann Donovan on 4th August 1835 in Lower Hawkesbury. The couple would contribute four children to the Woodbury line.

The eldest of Richard and Sally's children, Richard Woodbury (II), married Jane Neal on 16th October 1837 in Mangrove Creek. In all, Richard (II) and Jane Woodbury would have twelve children over the next twenty-four years.

Rebecca Woodbury, the sixth child of Richard and Sally, married William Craft on 24th April 1837 in Lower Portland. William and Rebecca Craft would have ten children.

Ann Woodbury married James Craft in Gosford on 27th July 1840 and bore him seven children. After the death of James Craft in 1854, Ann married Adam Dovey on 9th February 1858 in Wollombi. Ann and Adam had no children together.

Jeremiah Woodbury married Maria Chaseling in February 1854 in Lower Mangrove and the couple would go on to have eight children, although one was stillborn.

On 16th June 1856 John Woodbury married Mary Ann Wells in Wollombi in the Hunter Valley. The small village of Wollombi was Mary Ann Wells' birthplace and the couple settled there to be close to her family, although they later moved back to the Hawkesbury and the Brisbane Waters areas. Through John Woodbury and his wife Mary Ann, a further four children would be added to the Woodbury line.

And Jane Woodbury married John Patience Cornwell in 1857 in Dungog, in the Hunter Valley and the couple lived with their three children in Dungog.

Of course, the same thing was happening within the Everingham extended family as grandchildren were born to Sally Woodbury's siblings. Together, the Everingham and Woodbury extended families became very prominent in the Hawkesbury, from Windsor to the Lower Hawkesbury.

Little George James Woodbury became an uncle at the tender age of just five months when his sister, Elizabeth Hibbs née Woodbury, gave birth to a baby girl on 21st May 1832. George's new niece was given the same name as her mother, Elizabeth Hibbs. By his tenth birthday, George had become an uncle to no fewer than thirteen children – five from his eldest sister, Elizabeth: Elizabeth (b. 1832),

William (b. 1833), George (b. 1835), Mary (b. 1837) and Sarah Rebecca (b. 1839). In addition, George was also uncle to four children from his sister Sarah: Joseph (b.1835), Elizabeth (b. 1836), Ann Matilda (b. 1839) and Jane (b. 1840). George's older brother, William, contributed three more nephews during George's first ten years: William Woodbury (II) (b. 1836), Matthew James (b. 1838) and James Joseph (b. 1840). Then, just a few months before George's tenth birthday his sister, Ann, provided another nephew, James (b. September 1841).

Notwithstanding the fact that George's older brother, Matthew James, had unexpectedly died in Laughtondale on the Hawkesbury on 23rd November 1835, at only seven years of age, the multiple branches of the Woodbury family would continue to grow beyond George's tenth birthday. Ultimately, George would be uncle to sixty-one people, although not all of them carried the Woodbury name because George's sisters, of course, took their husband's names.

Whilst Richard and Sally Woodbury would spend the rest of their lives at Mangrove Creek and at other places on the Hawkesbury, it would be these next generations, their children and their grandchildren, who would carry the Woodbury name further afield, some moving eastwards to Brisbane Waters on the central coast of New South Wales in and around Gosford, others into the Hunter Valley around Wollombi, and others yet further north into the region known as the northern tablelands, west of the Great Dividing Range.

One day in 1838, Richard Woodbury took his wife Sally out to the deck behind their house at Mangrove Creek. As they sat there drinking their tea, Richard floated the idea of selling their fifty-acre grant at Upper Mangrove Creek.

"I don't think we need it anymore, Sal," he said. "We're secure on this lease of the church reserve land and we're not making full use of both parcels of land."

Sally sipped her tea and thought about the idea.

"We've only got four children living at home now," Richard continued. All the others are married, except for Jeremiah. But he is well established on the land that he is leasing further upstream near Cumberland Reach and he'll marry in time too."

"Land's always valuable," Sally said at last. "I remember you saying how Andrew Thompson always told you to accumulate property. So, why sell it?"

"Yes," Richard agreed, "land is valuable, but by selling it we'd be capitalising on our assets and be in a position to make other investments if something comes up. Besides, the fifty-acre grant is not great land."

Sally sighed. She remembered having the same discussion more than twenty years earlier, back in Windsor, when Richard's propensity to pursue increased prosperity through business deals had brought them undone. She pursed her lips but did not say anything. Richard was her husband, the head of the family, and ultimately, her role was to defer to him, so she silently nodded her assent in agreement. Then getting up from the deck, she took Richard's hand and together they walked back to the house.

The fifty-acre land grant at Upper Mangrove Creek was sold in 1838 and Richard used part of the proceeds to purchase ten acres of land at Cumberland Reach from his brother-in-law, Matthew James Everingham (II).

At least it's good land and it's close to my brother's land, Sally thought to herself.

Richard, however, considered the ten acres at Cumberland Reach to be simply an investment, and the land was left fallow while the family continued to live near Sugee Bag Creek. Sally was happy living there, surrounded by all her married children within the Mangrove Creek catchment area. She loved having four of her children still living at home too —John (sixteen), Ann (fourteen), Jane (twelve), and George (eight).

It was during a family gathering at the Sugee Bag Creek home when everyone was sitting outside in the winter sunshine that Richard spoke to his sons about what he saw as the perceived financial benefits of becoming involved in river transportation and shipping along the Hawkesbury. Sally listened apprehensively, hoping her sons would be more prudent with their investments than her husband had been.

"We're people of the river," Richard told them. "This river's the lifeblood of the settlers from Windsor to Broken Bay. My first employer in this country, Andrew Thompson, saw that twenty years ago and made a fortune out of shipping up and down the Hawkesbury, even as far as Sydney."

"And you think shipping on the river's still a profitable business to get involved in?" William asked.

"Of course it is," his father replied, "even more so than in Thompson's day. Your mother and I were in Sydney a couple of months ago. We travelled down on one of the new steamers. They unload at Cockle Bay and then the produce is taken by carts to Haymarket, although they sell much more than just hay there."

Sally remembered that trip to Sydney fondly. It was the first time she had ever seen Sydney.

"You'd be amazed at the things they sell there," she told them. Bales of hay and grass, of course, but also fish and crabs, barrels of salted meat, live pigs, donkeys, cows, all kinds of leather goods, fabric, apples, oranges, figs, grapes, melons, and every kind of vegetable you could imagine. The melons were wonderful — green on the outside but red and watery on the inside and so sweet."

"And big," Richard added, indicating their size with his hands. "Bigger than a man's head."

"We bought one of those melons," Sally added. "They have a lot of black seeds inside them. I'm drying the seeds and hoping I can grow them in the small garden up behind the house."

"I'd like to see that market," Jeremiah said. "It sounds like an interesting place."

"It is," Sally said, "but oh-so noisy, with all the sellers calling out, trying to attract buyers."

Richard tapped his pipe on his heel to clear the bowl, refilled it and drew on it as he lit the tobacco, which caused a short outburst of coughing.

"You should give up that pipe," Sally said. "It'll be the death of you!"

Richard looked at her for a moment but ignored her comment and turned back to his sons.

"That Sydney market's the reason farming along the Hawkesbury is changing," he said. "The wheat and corn farms are still here, of course, but many orchards and large vegetable farms are now just as important to the economy as they are."

Jeremiah nodded. "Yeah, I've seen ships on the river loaded with fruit and vegetables headed both to Windsor and downriver to Sydney."

"Steamers?" Richard asked.

"Still some using sail, especially those headed to Windsor. But steamers are starting to replace them heading downriver."

"That's also a result of the changing farming trends," Richard said. "With wheat or corn you can take your time getting it to market. But fruit and vegetables don't stay fresh very long, so you need to get them to market much quicker — most boats using sail are too slow to transport them to Sydney. Half the load would be unmarketable by the time it got there."

"There are still some very fast sail boats," William countered. "Some of the new cutters are as fast as steamers, if the conditions are right."

"Yes," Richard nodded, "but steamers are more reliable — not so dependent on the right conditions."

William went to the house and came back with bottles of beer for everyone.

"Not as good as the Kable & Woodbury Ale we used to brew in Windsor," Richard said with a smile as he sipped on his bottle, "but it'll do, I suppose."

All the men had a good laugh at that.

"You know," Sally said, "I love this river. It seems like it's part of me."

"It's part of all of us," her husband replied. "Our children have been brought up on the river. Really, they've never lived anyplace where they've been out of sight of it — and they've certainly spent enough time on it in the boats."

"Maybe you're right," William said. "Maybe we do need to think about using the river to make a living."

Within eighteen months, Jeremiah and William were both operating cargo and passenger ships on the Hawkesbury, from Windsor through Broken Bay to Sydney. Jeremiah bought and operated the seventy-ton steamer, the *John & Herbert*, whilst William employed an adept shipwright to build a fast single masted cutter for him which he named the *William & Mary* after himself and his wife, Mary Ann, a lady of Irish descent.

Although she was a sailing vessel, given the right conditions, the *William & Mary* was regarded as one of the fastest vessels travelling to Sydney, on one occasion registering a time of one hour and twenty-five minutes from Broken Bay to Sydney, a record that would stand for some time. Both vessels carried fruit and vegetable produce, as well as passengers, between Windsor and Sydney and, on the return run they carried all manner of produce needed by the people of the Hawkesbury and Windsor. They often also carried building materials — timber, bricks, tiles and iron roofing sheets.

Economic survival in the colony, however, became increasingly difficult. Severe drought hit the colony in 1838–1840 and necessitated the importation of wheat and that, combined with the downturn in the wool industry, again largely caused in by the drought, brought the colony's productivity almost to a standstill. The British financial crisis of 1839 resulted in the retreat of investment from the colony, slowing capital inflow to a trickle. Land prices slumped and falling commodity prices caused an upsurge of insolvencies amongst the settlers. This downturn was the first real economic depression in the colony and precipitated the first wave of bank failures in the country.

The depression of the 1840s brought unemployment on an unprecedented scale and bankrupted hundreds of businesses. Even breweries went to the wall, defying the axiom that you can't go bust if you own a brewery. The government began encouraging free immigration, believing the newcomers would bring capital and stimulate expansion within the colonies, thereby boosting consumption and investment, yet the initiative had quite the opposite effect. Instead, it glutted the labour market, as free workers competed with ticket-of-leave convicts. A prominent entrepreneur and businessman, John Hosking, convinced a bank to lend him more money than anyone else could borrow, for no other reason than that he was already the richest man in the country. Partly because of his perceived wealth, in 1842, Hosking was the first man elected to the office of Mayor of Sydney. However, the depression brought him down when he fell into bankruptcy part way through his first term of office and also brought down the bank that had lent him the money.

By 1844, Richard and Sally were once again in an unsustainable financial position. To meet the demands of their creditors, Richard sold his house and both properties near Sugee Bag Creek as well as the ten-acre property at Cumberland Reach, near Sackville.

The New South Wales colonial government refused to bail out the banks financially, but it did open up new grants of Crown Land to settlers who could show hardship caused by the depression. Late in 1844, Richard Woodbury was granted sixty acres of land at Bathurst Reach, about two miles up-river from Wiseman's Ferry, and there Richard and Sally and the young unmarried Woodbury children started over again from scratch. Richard was sixty-seven years of age and Sally was fifty-one. They built a stone house on the land, although they later sold the property to their son William.

One of the unexpected social consequences of the depression of the 1840s was the significant slow-down in marriages as young men prudently decided that they were not able to support a family. Ann Woodbury had married James Craft in mid-1840, just before the depression hit the colony, but Jeremiah, who had already moved out of the family home, would not marry until 1854. George waited until 1855, John until 1856 and Jane until 1857. George, John and Jane lived in the house at Bathurst Reach until each of them married. Sally and Richard also lived there until Richard passed away on 6th June 1867, at the age of ninety years. He was buried in the Laughtondale cemetery, his death certificate having been signed by his youngest son, George James Woodbury.

It was after Richard's funeral, as the extended family adjourned to a local teahouse for refreshments, that Sally's daughter, Rebecca, and her husband, William Craft, took her aside.

"Mother," Rebecca said, "now that Father's gone, William and I think you should come and live with us at Mangrove Creek. You've always loved living there."

"Oh, I couldn't do that," Sally replied. "You've got your own growing family and I wouldn't want to become an intruder."

"Don't be silly, Mother," Rebecca protested. "We'd build you your own little house next to ours. You'd be quite independent but, at the same time, part of our family."

In August 1867, Sally moved into a small stone house built for her on the Craft family property. She would live there until her own death on 29th March 1874, at the age of eighty-one years. After her death, her body was taken downriver to Wisemans Ferry on William's cutter the *William & Mary*, followed by a sad cortege of small boats carrying her grieving children and their families. There, in the Laughtondale cemetery, Sally was laid to rest alongside her husband.

After the internment, most of the Woodbury family retired for refreshments at a local teahouse-tavern in Wisemans Ferry where they reflected on the life and times of their parents — the good times and the hard ones, the happy and the sad.

"Do you remember when those escaped convicts broke into the house at Gunderman and almost killed Father?" Sarah asked the group.

Everyone nodded and remarked about their father's long recovery and how that had led to his resigning as District Constable.

"You saved Father's life that night, William," John said, "and probably Mother's life as well."

"It was the first time I'd ever used that gun," William replied. "It nearly knocked me off my feet when I fired it."

Everybody laughed thinking about the young boy almost being knocked down by the recoil from the shotgun.

"They had some difficult years didn't they?" Jane said. "All those times they had to start over. The bank collapse in the forties was the worst. They lost everything then, but they rebuilt their lives and provided for us."

"But there were good times too," Rebecca added. "The weddings were the best. Especially George and Sarah's wedding. What a night that was!"

Suddenly everyone was talking at once, laughing and enjoying their recollections of happy marriages. All except Sarah, known as Annie. Her marriage had not been such a happy one.

Richard Jnr called for glasses of ale all round and, when they were served, he stood and raised his glass.

"Here's to our mother and our father," he said, "God-fearing people and wonderful parents who always did their very best for their children in difficult times. May they rest in peace."

Fig. 2. The grave of Richard Woodbury and Sarah Elizabeth (Sally) Woodbury née Everingham at the Laughtondale cemetery. Note: this headstone has been placed by later descendants of Richard and Sally and it is the belief of this author that the date of Richard's birth, shown as 1781, is incorrect and that it should be 1777 (see p.5 & p.11).

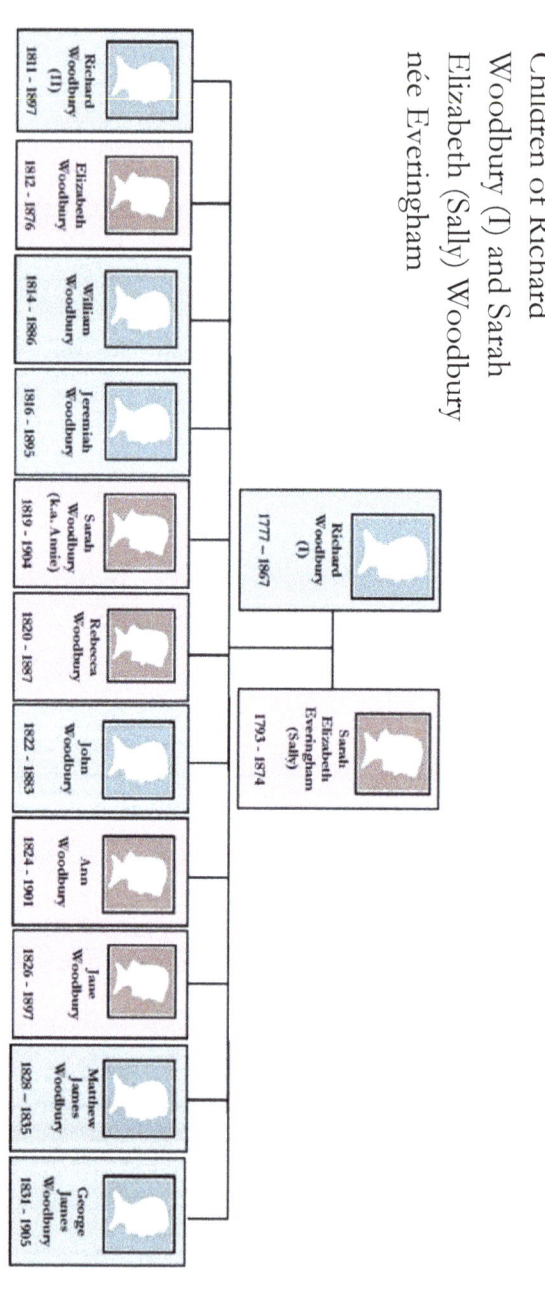

5
(1852 – 1872)

Johann Georg Schupp was born in born in Bornich, Rhein-Lahn-Kreis, Rhineland-Palatinate, Germany, in 1810 and his wife, Anna Katharina, was born in the same region about 1816. The couple arrived in Sydney, together with their four young children, on board the German immigrant ship *Reihersteig* on 5th August 1852. At the time of the family's arrival, Johann was aged forty-two and Anna thirty-six. Their children were Phillip Henry aged seven, Anna Elizabeth aged six, Phillip Toachim aged five, and Eva Magbalen, aged three.[1]

After the family arrived in Sydney their surname changed from Schupp to Schoupp, pronounced "Shop". It was not uncommon for names to be changed during the immigration process. Officials may have recorded the names they were told using phonetic transcriptions of what they thought was the correct spelling. Phonetic spelling, foreign accents, and bad handwriting can easily introduce errors into written records. Furthermore, once a misspelled name is entered into official documentation the error can, for the purposes of consistency or convenience, be perpetuated in the writing of subsequent records. It is also possible that the family may have deliberately changed the spelling to anglicise their name and make it more palatable to the people of their new land. That latter possibility may be given some veracity by the fact that, in Australia, Anna Katharina Schupp was known as Catherine Schoupp.

The *Reihersteig* that brought the Schupp family to Sydney was on its maiden voyage. It was a brave undertaking for a family with four young children to sail to the other side of the world in such a small vessel and this decision certainly displayed an adventurous and fearless spirit.

After disembarking on the Sydney wharf, Johann Schoupp sought out a cart driver and, in his broken English, asked to be taken to the cheapest accommodation in town.

"Do y' 'ave money?" the cart driver asked.

"I have English shillings," Catherine replied, her English being somewhat better than that of her husband.

"That'll work for me, luv. It'll be three shillin's."

Being totally new to the country, the family did not realise they were being taken for a ride in more ways than one. Three shillings was an outrageous price to pay for such a short ride.

"Me name's Thomas," the cart driver said by way of introduction as he loaded their luggage, and Catherine then introduced the family to him, still using the "Schupp" pronunciation of their name

"So, what's brought y' t' New South Wales?" the cart driver asked as they made their way up George Street.

"My husband is a miner," Catherine said. "We're hoping to be rich."

The cart driver threw his head back and laughed.

"Hah! Aren't we all, luv?" he said. "Where are y' headin' t' try yer luck?"

"Where… is… the… gold?" Johann managed to ask in his stammering English, and again the cart driver broke into loud laughter.

"Mate," he said, "do y' think I'd be drivin' this bloody cart if I knew where the gold were?"

As the cart driver helped unload their luggage in front of a small, decrepit guest house at the top end of George Street, he pulled Johann aside and spoke to him.

"My advice, mate, would to be forget about the gold," he said. "For every one o' them that finds gold there's thousands that don't. If I were you, I'd head north, to a place called Tiengha, near Inverell. I 'ear tell there's a few prospectors workin' the area and word is it looks like it might become a good place for minin'. Not gold, mind y', but maybe other metals 'nd perhaps even diamonds. Prospectin' is jist gittin' started up there, but it could turn quite profitable, 'specially if y' git in early, or so I 'ear."

"Thank you, Mr Thomas," Johann replied.

As the cart driver returned to the wharf in search of more customers, he threw his head back and laughed again.

"Tiengha!" he said to himself when he was out of earshot. "Probably the arsehole of this country. 'nd a family like that's gonna double the population. Hah!"

Catherine Schoupp had not heard the cartman's description of Tiengha as he had driven away, but had she heard him, she would have found herself in full agreement after arriving there. Tiengha was not a town, or even a settlement, but merely an ill-defined district located on the northern tablelands of New South Wales about twenty miles south of Inverell. Tiengha is an aboriginal word meaning *"flat"* or "*level*". Had the aboriginal people also included the words *"dry and dusty"*, they would have encapsulated the district's appearance accurately in those four words. With all due respect to the good people of today's small township, renamed Tingha, many would say this description still stands. In fairness, however, it must be said that there would come a day, long after Johann and Catherine first surveyed the barren landscape, when the mining industry would make Tiengha a significant settlement — for a time.

Tiengha Station had been established in 1841 when Sidney Hudson Darby and his partner J H Goldfinch took up a grant of 80,000 acres and called it the "Tiengah Run". From the Hunter Valley, Darby and Goldfinch, together with their wives, children, nannies, servants and labourers, had driven bullock carts carrying loads of adzed timber ready for the construction of the station homestead, along with everything else required to meet all their perceived needs — food supplies for six months, tools, saddles, harnesses, furniture and a piano. The bullock carts dragged all this across the Great Dividing Range in a journey that took six months to an unknown destination on the northern tablelands of New South Wales.

What Darby and Goldfinch thought when they arrived and surveyed their "run" is not recorded for us, but we can safely assume they must have been men of some fortitude, for they did decide to stay. Perhaps they simply thought driving the bullock carts back across the range was too much trouble even to contemplate.

Twelve years later, Johann and Catherine Schoupp stood in the same place, staring at the desolate and inhospitable landscape.

"Are you sure this is the right place, Johann?", Catherine asked. "Who can possibly live in a place like this?"

Johann continued to survey the surrounding area — flat, dry and dusty as far as the eye could see.

"It's the right place," he replied, "but I didn't expect it to be as barren as this. There's nothing here for us."

"To think we left Germany to come to this place!" Caroline cried as she began to weep.

"We'll go back to Inverell," Johann said. "We'll see if we can find a house to rent until we decide what to do."

The Schoupp family took a lease on a fifty-acre property at Brodies Plains, some ten miles east of Inverell, and Johann tried to establish himself as a wheat farmer. He supplemented his farming efforts with itinerant work in Inverell and some part-time prospecting and fossicking in the streams around Inverell. In the process, he even found a few sapphires. Life remained a struggle, however, and Catherine frequently lamented leaving Germany. Part of the struggle had its roots in the fact that the family was culturally and socially rejected by the people of the very small township of Inverell. In town, Johann was called "Fritz" in an unfriendly tone, and the Schoupp family, with their limited English and heavy accents, were considered foreigners and interlopers by the townspeople.

"Bloody Huns! Go back where y' bloody came from!" the ethnocentric locals would say to Johann and his family when they went to Inverell for supplies.

Johann and Catherine and their children were culturally different, and their religious practices were different too, for they were Lutherans.

Lutheranism embraces the standard affirmations of classic Protestantism, including the repudiation of papal and ecclesiastical authority in favour of accepting the Bible as the sole and infallible source of authority for Christian faith and practice. In accordance with the teachings of Martin Luther and the catechism of the Lutheran Reformation, the Lutheran church reduced the number of sacraments from seven to two — retaining only baptism and the Eucharist as the "means of grace" or sacraments of Lutheran belief and practice. As Lutherans, the Schoupp family found themselves uncomfortable within both the Church of England and the Wesleyan Methodist Church and, by default, gravitated towards the Salvation Army. It was not a perfect fit for them, for they missed the sacraments of baptism and the Eucharist which the Salvation Army did not practise. However, all things being considered, it seemed this was the church that most closely accommodated their Lutheran beliefs and practices.

The Salvation Army in Inverell at that stage was a very fledgling religion and one that, in those early days, experienced significant opposition from local authorities. Local councils employed a person in the role of Inspector of Nuisances, and the Inverell Inspector of Nuisances often confronted the Salvation Army's open-air meetings and moved them on. In Bingara, some thirty miles west of Inverell and not far from the Myall Creek Station, an Inspector of Nuisances served the local Salvation Army with a summons for being 'the boss nuisance in the district', a charge which the soldiers of the Salvation Army in Bingara wore as a badge of honour.

Things remained difficult for the Schoupp family at Brodies Plains until an amazing transformation came upon the district in the early 1870s — the first viable tin deposits in the colony were discovered near Tiengha and the nearby village of Elsmore. Prospectors rushed to the area and the district population swelled, with diggers hoping to cash in on the mining of readily accessible tin. New businesses sprung up in Inverell to support the mining communities in villages like Tiengha, Elsmore, Bingara and others.

The sudden influx of newcomers also helped the Schoupp family gain greater acceptance within the wider community, probably because more than half of the newcomers were Chinese. The racist and redneck locals looked at Johann Schoupp and his family and thought, *Well, Fritz and his family have been here a long time. They're not Aussies, but they're better than all those bloody Chinese.* Thereafter, Catherine found the good ladies of Inverell more willing to talk with her and when Johann was called "Fritz", it was more often said with a smile and a wave, as a term of endearment. The family had gained a certain level of acceptance, albeit at the expense of the Chinese.

The discovery of viable tin deposits in 1870 piqued the interest of Johann Schoupp, of course, and he began considering a return to the one industry that he really knew — mining. It was a matter that had to be discussed with Catherine, however.

"It's the one thing I know, Cath," he said to her over dinner. "It's in my blood."

But Catherine remembered her first and only sighting of Tiengha when they arrived in the district, back in 1853, and was not keen to take a second look.

"I remember Tiengha, Johann," she said. "It's so dry and dusty, almost like a desert. I don't think I could live out there."

"It's been renamed," Johann said. "It's called Tingha now."

"Tiengha or Tingha," Catherine replied. "Does a name change make the place any more liveable?"

"But we're struggling to survive here at Brodies Plains," Johann countered. "And that's because I'm not cut out to be a farmer. I don't know enough about farming — and there's good money to be made at Tingha."

Catherine sighed and refilled their cups with tea before answering.

"There's the children to think of, Johann," she said. "What's at Tingha for them — and for me too for that matter? I like it here at Brodies and, with the way the townspeople are accepting us now, it finally feels like home."

"The boys are not children anymore, Cath," Johann retorted. "They're well into their twenties and they deserve the opportunity to get work in the mines too and set themselves up for married life."

Catherine and Johann reached an uneasy truce before retiring for the night. Nothing had been decided, but they were both aware that the matter would be revisited in the days, weeks and months to come. Catherine lay awake that night, reflecting on the fact that she had held her husband at Brodies Plains for many years, resisting his innate urge to return to the mining industry. She was grateful for those years at Brodies Plains but realised she would be unable to hold him there for much longer. And she wondered whether she had any right to do so.

In early 1872, something else occurred which would have a long-lasting impact on the Schoupp family. New neighbours moved to Brodies Plains and leased the property adjoining their own. The surname of the new neighbours was Woodbury.

1. NSW Assisted Immigration Passenger Lists, 1828-1896

6
(1855 – 1873)

George James Woodbury, the youngest child of Richard Woodbury (I) and Sarah Elizabeth (Sally) Woodbury née Everingham, had married Sarah Elizabeth Pate Charter on 10th June 1855 in the Wesleyan Methodist Church in Windsor.[1] After the marriage ceremony, the entire Woodbury extended family returned to their parents' house at Bathurst Reach where the dancing and celebrations extended throughout the night.

Sarah Elizabeth Pate Charter was seventeen on her wedding night and George was ten years older. Sarah was born on 5th December 1837 in Ashwell, Hertfordshire, England and had arrived in New South Wales with her family on board the *William Turner* on 5th October 1841. Thomas and Elizabeth Charter were free settlers who brought with them their three young children, Thomas, aged four, Sarah, aged three, and Cornelius, aged one.

After the death of Richard Woodbury (I), George's father, George and Sarah remained at the Bathurst Reach house to care for George's mother, Sally, until she moved to the Mangrove Creek property of William Craft and her daughter Rebecca. They then took over the Bathurst Reach house and farm and continued to live there until 1869. Ultimately, they would have eleven children. Seven of the first eight children were born at the Bathurst Reach house— Matthew William, born 23rd August 1856, Caroline, born 20th December 1857, Aquilla, born 3rd May 1859, James Joseph, born 26th August 1862, Gabriel, born 1st January 1864, Solomon, born 1st July 1865 and Abel, born 10th May 1867.

The couple's fourth child, Martha, had been born on 26th August 1860 during a short sojourn at Wollombi in the Hunter Valley where George's sister Sarah, known as Annie, was living.

In 1869, George and his family relocated to the Brisbane Waters district on the central coast of New South Wales to be closer to George's siblings, Richard (II), Anne and John. It was during their time at Brisbane Waters that George's wife, Sarah, gave birth to two more children — John Amos, born 1870 and Emma, born 1871.

George and Sarah had no deck at Brisbane Waters but, had there been one, that is where they would have sat on a summer's evening in January 1872. Instead, it was at the table after dinner that George raised the subject of the family "moving north", as he put it.

"You mean around Copeland where your sister lives?" his wife asked.

"No, although I do feel sorry for Annie. Her husband, Joseph Bridge, always was a restless spirit, constantly wanting to move from one district to another and often leaving Annie alone to care for their children for long periods. Eventually, he deserted her completely and I don't know where he is now. Annie's had a hard life, but her daughter's looking after her now at Copeland."

"Yes," Sarah replied. "I remember when we visited Wollombi almost ten years ago when Annie was living there. I'll never forget how our Martha was born there. Annie's husband, Joseph, was not there then and Annie was very unhappy. Not surprising given her circumstances."

Unfortunately, for Annie Woodbury, or perhaps fortunately, her life with Joseph Bridge at Wollombi had not lasted long. Within three years of arriving there, they had separated and, by 1845 Joseph Bridge was living with Mary Ann Carpenter and had started a second family. No divorces were granted in the early years of the colony — everyone across the spectrum of society argued against divorce. Men argued that it undermined the subservient role of women in marriage, whilst women, for their part, argued that it undermined their security. Predictably, the church condemned divorce as an abhorrent repudiation of Christian beliefs and practices.

In 1873, an inequitable provision for divorce on the grounds of adultery was introduced in New South Wales. The legislation was discriminatory in as much as it allowed a husband to petition for divorce on the grounds of his wife's adultery. A wife's petition for divorce, however, had to prove not only adultery on the part of her husband, but also cruelty, drunkenness and violence.

Desertion was not an acceptable claim for divorce and women such as Annie Bridge née Woodbury, deserted and without adequate grounds for divorce, could not legally remarry or receive any help from the state towards the care of the children. They were left to their own initiative and the help of friends and family. Annie Bridge eventually chose to live with her daughter, Sarah, who had married John Saxby and lived at Bowman, just north of Copeland, NSW.

George sat lost in thought, as he slowly lit his pipe.

"No, I'm not thinking of moving to Copeland," he said eventually.

"Where, then?" Sarah asked.

"I'm thinking further north, to the district they call the northern tablelands. They say the land up there west of the Great Divide is good farming land with rich dark soil, and that there's a developing mining industry which would be a good back-up if the farming proved difficult."

"That's a long way to move with ten children, George," Sarah replied, "especially with Emma being so young, but we can do it, I suppose, if you think it'd be a good move for our family."

The decision to move north was made and, six months later, the family moved north. They found themselves just south of the northern border of the Colony of NSW at a place called Brodies Plains, about ten miles east of the settlement town of Inverell. At Brodies Plains George leased land which he would eventually buy, next door to a property where a German family was trying to eke out a living growing wheat. Sarah at first thought they would have been better off living in Inverell town, but the town was built within an almost horseshoe-shaped bend of the Macintyre River, and George had heard people say the Macintyre frequently flooded.

"We'll be better off out here high and dry at Brodies," he said. And that German family living on the neighbouring property seem like good people. I think we'll be able to get on well with them. It's not that far from town anyway."

"You Woodburys seem to be taking over the Hawkesbury. There are bloody Woodburys everywhere now! Y' can't go anywhere without fallin' over one of 'em," said Charlie Doyle, jokingly.

It was August 1876 and Charlie Doyle had chanced upon one of his neighbours from upriver, John Woodbury, at the marketplace in Windsor. The two decided to share lunch and a chat at the tavern in George Street. As they sat eating and enjoying an ale on the veranda overlooking Thompson Square, the conversation had turned to the Woodbury family.

"Well, we're a big family, you know," John Woodbury replied, after taking a sip of his ale. "My grandparents had eleven kids, and my own parents had twelve. Pretty much the same with all my father's brothers and sisters – they all had big families."

"Y'all must be breeding like bloody rabbits," Doyle said with a laugh.

John Woodbury allowed himself a smile but said nothing, instead taking another mouthful of his ale.

"And there's the Everinghams too," Doyle continued. "There's nearly as many of them as there are Woodburys. They're part of your family too, aren't they?"

"Yeah," John replied. "My grandmother was an Everingham. She came as a convict on the Second Fleet and married Matthew Everingham who had arrived as a convict on the First Fleet. They were well known in the Hawkesbury until their death. And now my brothers and sisters and I, and my cousins, are all working on the next generation," he said with a chuckle. "The Everinghams are doing the same, I suppose."

"Like I said, y' breed like bloody rabbits," Doyle repeated as he refilled his pipe, having finished his lunch and pushed his plate aside. "My younger brother, Adam, got back from a prospecting trip up north a few months back and he said he saw a Woodbury beating on the big drum for the Salvation Army in the main street of Inverell."

"That'd be my Uncle George," John replied, "or maybe his son, Matthew. They all moved up to that area a few years back."

"Thought all your family were Wesleyan Methodists?" Doyle asked.

"Some are — a lot are, I guess," said John. "Seems Uncle George and his family have found their own way though."

George and his family had indeed found their own way. When they arrived in the district at Brodies Plains, the young settlement town of Inverell seemed, to George at least, to be a rather unruly frontier town. Squatters had moved into the district from about the 1840s, establishing large sheep and cattle stations, but it was the discovery of tin in 1871, less than a year before the arrival of George and his family, that had triggered a rapid increase in Inverell's population. Not quite a gold rush, but tin was valuable enough and readily available, so large numbers of prospective miners flocked to the area, intent on joining the tin-mining industry at Elsmore, not far from Inverell. Many were Chinese, but others came from Cornwall, from Ireland

and from other parts of Europe, whilst yet others were failed diggers from the Australian gold fields. In this melting-pot, disputes and violence were common occurrences and George realised that this unruliness was largely fuelled by an excessive indulgence in alcohol. The fractious and rowdy nature of the town was yet another reason George decided to settle his family some distance out of town at Brodies Plains. Although in his earlier days George had enjoyed a glass of ale now and then — his father, after all, had been one of the colony's first brewers — he was unsettled by what he saw as the abusive repercussions of alcohol in the community where he now lived.

When George spoke to his neighbour, Johann Schoupp, about the negative impact that alcohol abuse was having on the local community, Johann invited him to attend Salvation Army open-air meetings in Inverell. The Salvation Army was a church that had general adherents, but committed members were referred to as soldiers.

"The Salvation Army demands that its soldiers totally abstain from alcohol. I think you'd fit in well there. They're good-living people."

Soon thereafter, George swore off alcohol for the rest of his life and the entire family became zealous soldiers of the Salvation Army in Inverell.

The Salvation Army had always been, and would always be, not only a Christian church spreading the gospel of Jesus Christ, although it certainly saw that as its primary mission, but also an organisation concerned with reaching out to help all those in need of support. As such, it had both an evangelical as well as a social welfare mission. In the mid-20th Century, the territorial leader of the Australian Eastern and Papua New Guinea Salvation Army Territory, Lieutenant-Colonel John Gowans, would summarise the mission of the Salvation Army, a mission that has not really changed since its inception, in the following way — "Save souls, Grow saints, and Serve suffering humanity." Although these words would not be enunciated until well after the death of both Johann Schoupp and George Woodbury, it nonetheless stood at the core of the Salvation Army's mission in those earlier times. And in the mind of George Woodbury, perhaps the one group he most associated with that suffering humanity was the indigenous population.

The original inhabitants of the northern tablelands were the indigenous people of the Kamilaroi Nation (pronounced Gamilaroi), the second largest aboriginal nation in New South Wales, after the land of the Waradjuri Nation that lies further south and west of the Blue Mountains. In the central north of New South Wales, the Kamilaroi people enjoyed fertile soil, fresh running rivers with plentiful fish stock, yam beds, and abundant game in the bushland.

From the very commencement of white settlement in 1788, the spread of non-indigenous settlement across New South Wales gradually pushed aboriginal people off their land and away from their food sources, often into a state of near starvation. In many places, perhaps all, the rise of white settlement towns pushed the aboriginal people beyond the town limits where they became fringe-dwellers, living in camps — sad places for sad families, for dispossessed people, for the destitute, the hungry, the broken-hearted, and those who had nowhere else to go.

In this regard, Inverell was not unique amongst the townships of New South Wales. George had observed the same sad phenomenon in the Hawkesbury where he had lived in his early years. Indeed, many would have said that the Woodbury family in the Hawkesbury contributed to that phenomenon, and George would not have argued with that. Across Australia, aboriginal people were reduced to the status of fringe-dwellers outside town limits.

What cannot be denied, however, is the fact that many of the good people of Inverell in those early days remembered the Myall Creek massacre which had occurred in June 1838, just twenty miles from Inverell. By the time George Woodbury and his family arrived at Brodies Plains in 1872, the Myall Creek massacre was still talked about, not with shame by some, but with a real sense of satisfaction.

In the late 1830s, gangs of marauding stockmen roamed the district slaughtering any aboriginal people they could find. On 9th June 1838, a group of eleven stockmen, all convicts or ex-convicts apart from the leader of the group, John Henry Fleming, arrived at the Myall Creek station. They rode up to a gathering of station huts where a group of approximately thirty aboriginal people who belonged to the Kamilaroi Nation sat. When the stockmen rode into their camp, the aborigines fled into a convict supervisor's hut, pleading for his protection. The convict supervisor asked the raiding stockmen what they intended to do with the aboriginal people. Fleming replied, "We're going to take them over the back of the range and frighten them." The stockmen then entered the hut, tied the aborigines together with a long rope and led them away. They took them to a gully about a thousand yards to the west of the station and there they slaughtered every one of them — mostly women, children, and old men.

Testimony was later given at trial that the stockmen had decapitated the children and hacked the men and women to pieces with swords. After the massacre, the group dispersed and Fleming, the only free man involved, disappeared. Though the other members of the gang were ultimately arrested and faced trial on charges of murder, Fleming was never captured. He hid or was protected, probably in the Hawkesbury district where he later became a respected farmer, church warden and Justice of the Peace.

The Myall Creek massacre was notable as one of the very rare instances, and indeed the first instance, in which white Australians were executed for the murder of indigenous Australians. Seven members of the gang were publicly hanged for their part in the crime at Sydney Goal on 18th December 1838.

By the 1870s, when the Woodbury family settled at Brodies Plains, some white squatters in the district and some townspeople lived in relative peace with the local aborigines, albeit it in a form of segregated apartheid. Others, however, remained determined to eradicate aborigines from the district. Subsequent massacres in the district, and in many parts of Australia, went unreported. A distressing feature of community principles and morals of that era, not only in the Inverell district but across Australia, was the widely held belief that white Australians had every right to murder the indigenous people, without consequence.

For his part, George viewed the sad plight of the aboriginal fringe-dwellers as a situation brought about purely by the attitudes of white townspeople. Not only had the white people of the town driven the aborigines out of the town, but they had exacerbated the problem by providing them with access to alcohol which, George knew, was the root cause of much domestic violence amongst the aborigines. George hoped and prayed that his role within the Salvation Army might, in some small way, eventually lead to an improved lifestyle for his black brothers.

Within a year of the Woodbury family settling at Brodies Plains, it became clear to them that their neighbours, the Schoupp family, would be moving to Tingha. Ongoing discussions on the matter had occupied Johann and his wife Catherine for the best part of a year and came to a head in mid-1872.

"The miners at Tingha are making good money," Johann said to his wife, "while we're struggling to farm this property here at Brodies. We need to make the move before I'm too old to work in the mines."

Johann was now sixty-two years of age, and Catherine fifty-six. In Catherine's mind, her husband was already too old to be working in the mines. She remained reluctant to move but realised she had to relent when Johann made a proposal to her.

"You and the girls could stay here," he said. "I could go to Tingha with the boys. We could work in the mines and send money back to you here. I would visit when I could."

"No!" Catherine replied emphatically and without hesitation. "We're a family and I'll not separate our family. We go where you go."

When Johann told his neighbour, George Woodbury, that they would be moving, George wrapped his arms around him.

"We'll miss you, Johann — and all your family. But remember, you'll always be welcome in our home whenever you're in the district."

The two shook hands as they said their goodbyes.

"The Army in town will miss you too," George continued. "You've been a good soldier. In time, I'm sure there'll be a Salvation Army in Tingha and I'm sure you'll be a part of it. In the meantime, it's going to be difficult to sustain your faith. Come back and visit us as often as you need."

It would be 1888 before a small group of Salvationists formed the Tingha Salvation Army. Johann and Catherine Schoupp were founding soldiers of the Corps.

---

1. Limited family trees relating to the grandchildren of Richard Woodbury (I) and Sarah Elizabeth (Sally) Woodbury née Everingham are shown in this book as Appendix 1, pp. 236- 247

7
(1873 – 1901)

The Tingha that Catherine Schoupp remembered from her first sighting in 1852 had changed little. The area had been declared a "private town" in 1872 after the rich deposits of tin had been discovered, but "town" was merely an aspirational goal and far from a reality. It was still flat, dry and dusty, with few trees. True, some buildings had sprung up, almost all of which were timber slab buildings with timber or bark roofs, mostly with dirt floors. More than half of the buildings were commercial properties — general stores, saddleries, public houses etc. A small number of houses dotted the area around the stores, also built of slab timber and bark, and with dirt floors. Johann Schoupp and his two sons quickly built a small house in the same manner, close enough to the stores to be convenient, yet, at Catherine's insistence, as far away from the public houses as possible.

Fig. 1. Ruby Street, the main street of Tingha, c. 1873

Shortly after the family's arrival in Tingha, Catherine picked up a newspaper from the general store and read an article written by a regular correspondent from Tingha.

> *We have four public houses, seven stores, and two bakers' shops. About half the number would suffice. We have only one butcher's shop; the consequence is that the meat rules high.* [1]

Well, he got that right, Catherine thought to herself.

But Tingha, whilst remaining a frontier mining town, had grown exponentially since Pennyweight Joe, or Joseph Wills to give him his true name, had first discovered tin in the general area. Employers and acquaintances in the Inverell-Elsmore district had given Wills the nickname of Pennyweight Joe because of his small stature.

Wills was an itinerant shepherd, tending the flocks of pastoralists within the area, who found that this work gave him time and opportunity to prospect his shepherd's run, searching for gold which he never found. He did, however, find and collect other unidentified gems and geological specimens all of which he bundled up and sent to his brother-in-law, Frederick Clar De V'ries in London. Clar De V'ries had the specimens analysed and reported back to Wills that they included rubies, sapphires, and tin.

Wills thought nothing, or very little, about his discovery of tin and concentrated his amateur prospecting efforts on fossicking, hoping to find more rubies and sapphires. In 1870, however, whilst drinking in an Inverell hotel, he fell into conversation with a man named C. S. McGlew, a traveller from Sydney. McGlew, as it turned out, had been searching for commercial-grade tin deposits across northern New South Wales.

"I've got some bags o' tin at 'ome," Wills told him. "If y're interested, I'll sell y' a bag o' tin f' five shillin's."

On his return to Sydney McGlew had the tin sample smelted to test its value. Soon after he hurried back to Inverell and sought out Wills whom he persuaded to show him the area near Elsmore, a short distance east of Inverell, where the tin had been found. In June 1871, McGlew & Associates began commercially mining tin at Elsmore.

Wills, meanwhile, with renewed interest in tin, found another rich deposit not far from Elsmore which he somewhat naively showed to his pastoralist employer, Duncan Anderson. Anderson, whose interest had already been piqued by the successes of the McGlew tin-mining entity, quickly associated himself with a Sydney based mining magnate of the time, one Saul Samuel, and, in short order, two major mining companies were exploiting Wills's discoveries.

Although Pennyweight Joe had been the first to discover it in the general district, he did not discover tin in the district which would become known as Tingha. That honour went to two prospectors, a Mr Fearby and a Mr Millis, who found a rich deposit of tin on the banks of Copes Creek on the Tiengah Run. Without announcing their discovery, Fearby and Millis contrived to purchase as much of the Tiengah Run as they could. Messers Darby and Goldfinch, the owners, who were by now becoming disillusioned with their efforts to run stock on their property, quickly agreed to sell 240 acres at the junction of Cope's Creek and Darby's

Branch Creek to Fearby and Millis, who then formed the Britannia Tin Mining Company.

Anticipating that the success of their company would trigger a mining rush, Fearby and Mills then set about surveying a private town which they called Tingha where they would sell residential and business rights to those wishing to move to the area and make Tingha a town. The name, Tingha, was derived from the name Tiengah Run, but incorporated the word "tin" which was, after all, the reason for the town's existence. The area of this yet-to-be township continued to be known as the Cope's Creek Tin Field but, by 1872, the growing township was recognised as the private township of Tingha.

As for Pennyweight Joe, he was given a small lifetime annuity by the two companies who were mining at Elsmore on the tin deposits he had discovered, but he died in 1873 having received only one annuity payment. No thought was given by either of the mining companies to extending a bequest to his descendants. The headstone on his gave bears the words:

> *He paved the way for others' gains,*
> *And dies neglected for his pains.*

Fearby & Millis's expectation that their successful mining of tin at Tingha would trigger a rush of miners to their private town proved correct. Thousands of prospectors flocked to the area, all hoping to make their fortunes. Around thirty percent of them were Chinese prospectors. The other prospectors and citizens always viewed the large Chinese community in Tingha askance, as happened in other places too. The Chinatown area of Tingha had three joss houses, several Chinese gambling dens, opium dens and extensive Chinese owned market gardens. The Chinese population celebrated the Chinese New Year festival and Qingming (the festival of the dead), sometimes to the annoyance of the white, ethno-centric townspeople. All of this, together with the fact that most of the general stores were Chinese owned, threatened the perceived security and cultural legacy of the white populace and would be fundamental to forming views, in the new century, which would give rise to a policy known as the White Australia Policy.

Tingha and its forerunner, Tiengha Run, like most rural settlements in New South Wales, had been founded on aboriginal land in the mid-nineteenth century by Europeans intent on pursuing economic opportunities and paying little heed to the rights of indigenous Australians. In the early 19th century, the broader area was used for sheep grazing by colonial squatters who drove the aboriginal people off their land. With the discovery of tin, the small private hamlet of Tingah was established as a mining camp to accommodate and service the needs of miners. Aborigines had little place in this non-indigenous creation and, as elsewhere, were reduced to the status of fringe-dwellers on their own land.

When Johann and Catherine Schoupp arrived in Tingha with their family in August 1872, they found themselves late for the party. By then, up to a thousand prospectors were mining the readily available and clearly visible deposits of tin.

    "I told you we should have moved here last year, Cath," Johann said to his wife as they observed the intense mining activity around them.

Catherine, who had resisted Johann's innate desire to move to the mining fields for so many years, smiled at him indulgently.

"I'm sure there'll be enough tin to go around, Johann," she replied.

And there was. As long as prospectors confined their activities to outside Fearby & Millis's pegged area around the junction of Cope's Creek and Darby's Branch Creek, there was surface tin everywhere for the taking. The Schoupp family, working alongside other prospectors, were able to scoop up and bag tin with little more than a shovel. Johann and his two sons, Phillip Henry and Phillip Toachim, were making good money and they saved as much as they could by depositing their money in Inverell banks.

Yet, despite the extraordinary mining activity going on around the small hamlet, or perhaps because of it, Tingha remained a ramshackle frontier town frequently beset by the outbreaks of violence which often accompany a predominately male population indulging in excessive alcohol consumption. Although they were never attacked, Catherine and her younger daughter, Eva, felt unsafe in the unruly township, while their menfolk were at work during the day. Catherine and Johann's elder daughter, Anna Elizabeth had married James Hughes of Armidale and had settled in the Armidale district. To ease Catherine's fears, Johann would frequently take Eva and her, and sometimes also his two sons, to Brodies Plains to visit their good friends, George and Sarah Woodbury.

The promise of improved peace and order in Tingha came in May 1873 when the *Armidale Express & New England*

General Advertiser reported plans to bring a certain level of lawfulness to the district.

> *The respectable inhabitants of Tingha should throw up their hats and rejoice. The Police Commissioner has given instructions to Inspector Harrison to establish a police camp in the township to afford protection to the inhabitants against the ruffianly acts of the Forties and others of that ilk, and we believe tenders will be shortly called for the construction of suitable buildings for police quarters as well as a lock-up.* [2]

Like many political promises, however, the proposed police quarters and lock-up took some time to eventuate.

By the mid-1870s, more and more mines were cropping up all across the granite belt, and Tingha's population had grown to over two and a half thousand. It would continue to grow, reaching a peak of around eight thousand in the mid-1880s.

Notwithstanding the fact that Johann and Catherine were quite recurrent visitors to the home of their friends and former neighbours at Brodies Plains, George and Sarah Woodbury, by far the most frequent visitor was their elder son Phillip Henry. Phillip found there was something about the Woodbury family which kept drawing him back to Brodies Plains. Her name was Aquilla Woodbury, the third child, and second daughter, of George and Sarah Woodbury.

The well-established friendship between the Woodbury and Schoupp families was formally consolidated into a family relationship when Phillip Henry Schoupp married Aquilla Woodbury on 15th July 1879. Phillip was forty-two years of age at the time of their marriage and Aquilla was twenty — a considerable age difference, even in an era when men customarily sought out younger wives. In 1879, the Salvation Army in Inverell still had no building in which they could hold meetings and events such as marriages, so Phillip and Aquilla were married at the Woodbury family home at Brodies Plains in a ceremony solemnised by the senior member of the Inverell Salvation Army.

With the marriage of Phillip and Aquilla, of course, the family name of the ensuing branch of the Woodbury family changed to Schoupp. There would be many branches of the family retaining the Woodbury name, through Aquilla's six brothers and through many cousins in the extended Woodbury family. Yet Aquilla's children, and their descendants, whilst not bearing the Woodbury name, would nonetheless be descendants of the Woodbury ancestral line.

Aquilla, of course, accompanied her husband back to Tingha where Phillip had already constructed a small, rudimentary house close to his parents. Catherine, in particular, was delighted to have another female family member nearby in what was still very much, a frontier village — there was safety in numbers! In September 1881, Catherine and her son, Phillip, loaded their horse drawn cart and took a very pregnant Aquilla to Inverell where, on 13th September 1881, she was delivered of her first child, a daughter to whom they gave the name Sarah Elizabeth Pate Schoupp. Just two months later, Aquilla's oldest brother, Matthew William Woodbury married Jessie Ellen Seward, giving cause for yet another happy celebration at Brodies Plains for the now combined Woodbury and Schoupp families. In 1883, a second daughter, Emma Matilda, was born to Aquilla and Phillip Schoupp.

When the couple's third daughter was born on 18th May 1885, Phillip and Aquilla gave her the name Jessie Ellen. The names were chosen because Aquilla had grown very close to the wife of her brother, Matthew. Jessie Ellen Woodbury née Seward and Aquilla Schoupp née Woodbury were the closest of friends and Phillip was quite happy when Aquilla told him she would like to give their new daughter the same names as her sister-in-law.

"It's a great name for her," he said with a broad smile as he proudly nursed his newborn daughter. "I really like your brother Matthew, and his wife Jessie, although, next time, maybe a boy would be nice for us after three daughters."

"Keep trying," Aquilla said, laughing. "I'm sure we'll come up with a boy eventually."

Later that same year, 1885, the village of Tingha was the site of large-scale community celebrations when it was officially declared a "town".[3] The Tingha Brass Band led the celebrations under the baton of their proud Chinese bandmaster while Chinese firecrackers and red, white and blue bunting added to the festive atmosphere in Ruby Street, Tingha.

"What does it mean for us, Phillip?" Aquilla asked as they joined Johann and Catherine in the main street and sipped lemonade whilst most around them were drinking themselves into various states of inebriation.

"I'm not sure it means anything, Quill," her husband replied. "It could be that we'll get a little more attention from the councils in Inverell and Armidale. Maybe in the longer term it might lead to development here in Tingha and better facilities, but I wouldn't hold my breath waiting for that."

One issue upon which the declaration of Tingha as a town had absolutely no bearing was the propensity of Aquilla and Phillip to produce only daughters. Rhoda May Schoupp was born to Phillip and Aquilla in Inverell in 1887, giving the couple their fourth daughter.

It could be argued, however, that Tingha's coming of age as a town led to the formation of a small Salvation Army Corps there in 1888, with some members of the Tingha Brass Band forming the nucleus of the Tingha Salvation Army Band. They would remain a small but faithful group for many years, without a building in which to meet.

Throughout the 1880s, the Salvation Army in Inverell similarly had no building in which they could hold meetings, so they regularly held open-air meetings in Otho Street, the main street of Inverell. Gathered in a circle around their flag, with a few cornet players, women shaking and waving timbrels, and George Woodbury thumping on the big drum to keep time, the small group would sing hymns of praise before the speaker struggled to deliver the gospel story to passing townspeople — or at least to those who were sober.

By the late 1880s, Matthew Woodbury, the eldest son of George and Sarah Woodbury, had become a successful businessman in Inverell, after establishing the Inverell factory named *Soapworks* which proved to be a very lucrative business for him and his wife Jessie. Early in 1888, Matthew and Jessie Woodbury donated land at 35 Vivian Street, Inverell, for the building of the Salvation Army Citadel. The foundation stone carries the inscription *"This stone was laid, to the Glory of God, by M. W. Woodbury Esq, 7th December 1889."* The Citadel still stands on this site in Vivian Street. It has served the Inverell Salvation Army very well since 1890 and remains an imposing building to the glory of God.

The first eight decades of the nineteenth century were years of enormous growth in New South Wales and the other colonies. From a non-indigenous population of less than two thousand in 1800, that number had swelled to more than three million by 1890.

During the 1890s, however, the colonies were hit by a double crisis. The first was an economic crisis which began when the land boom bubble of the 1880s burst. Decreased foreign demand for Australian wool, Australia's core industry and main export earner, then sent the economy spiralling into a severe economic depression which, in time, would become global. Overseas investment ceased, unemployment soared and property prices collapsed as banks foreclosed on mortgages and unpaid leases were cancelled. Businesses in settlement towns failed, and many settlers faced homelessness and hunger. As fraud spread and public institutions began to fail, public confidence in the financial system collapsed and banks began closing their doors. Of the sixty-four banks operating in 1891, fifty-four had failed and closed by mid-1893, many of them permanently, and the colony's banking system was left in ruins.

The second crisis of the same decade came in the form of severe drought from 1895 to 1903 — a drought which is still considered the worst in Australia's history. This extensive drought was called "The Federation Drought," partly because it occurred at the time of Australia's federation as a nation in 1901, but also because it impacted such an extensive area of the continent.

In Inverell, the Salvation Army was one group that tried to serve the needs of the hungry, the homeless, and the unemployed by organising soup kitchens both within the town as well as in the camps of the indigenous fringe-dwellers.

At Brodies Plains, George Woodbury and his family were struggling to survive, as were all the people in the district. George was fifty-eight years of age when the economic collapse occurred and over sixty when the drought began to impact the area. Most of the Woodbury children had married and left home by that time, leaving only Solomon (born 1865) and the couple's youngest daughter, Emma (born 1871) at the family home at Brodies Plains. George and Sarah's youngest child, Rhoda, had died in infancy, born in 1873 and dying in 1874.

George and Sarah worked conscientiously in the Salvation Army soup kitchens and contributed vegetables from their own small vegetable garden which they struggled to maintain during the drought.

"We'll get through this, Sarah," George told his wife. "My parents went through this in the forties. They lost absolutely everything then, but they started over and rebuilt their lives. We'll do the same, if we must."

Sarah nodded.

"There are plenty worse off than us, George," she said. "Some around here would starve if it weren't for the soup kitchens."

George and Sarah worked in the Salvation Army soup kitchen in Inverell on several nights every week. In Tingha, together with a very small Salvation Army group, Johann and Catherine Schoupp donned their Salvation Army uniforms and distributed soup in Ruby Street to hungry and homeless miners. They would do so for many years.

Into these uncertain times, on 24th March 1892, a son, Solomon James, was born to Aquilla and Phillip Schoupp, their fifth child and first son. A second son, and the couple's last child, George Seth, was born on 15th July 1895.

The 1890s were not only a time of severe drought, and economic depression. They were also years during which the six colonies — New South Wales, Victoria, Queensland, Tasmania, South Australia, and Western Australia — struggled with the political imperative of coming together to form one nation.

By the mid to late 1880s, the six colonies all had their own parliaments, although each was still subject to the law-making power of the British Parliament. The colonies acted almost as six different countries, each having its own laws and its own militia serving as a defence force. They issued their own stamps and collected tariffs on goods that crossed their borders. They had even built railways using different gauges, complicating the transport of people and goods across their borders. Travelling by train between Melbourne and Sydney, for example, necessitated changing trains at Albury, for the Victorian gauge was wider than the New South Wales gauge and, as passengers struggled from one train to the other, on the platform at Albury, they had to queue to have the contents of their luggage inspected by customs officials. Freight had to be unloaded from Victorian trains and loaded onto New South Wales trains and vice-versa, which is why the railway platform in Albury remains the longest in Australia today. Because of the need for passengers to process through customs, it was considered impractical for the Victorian train to pull into one side of a shorter platform and the New South Wales train to pull into the other side. This would have allowed passengers simply to cross the platform to the other train, making the customs operations unmanageable. Instead, the trains pulled into the same side of the platform, end to end, and passengers had to traverse the length of the platform, passing through a customs inspection point as they did. The same disruption happened when crossing the border between New South Wales and Queensland, at Wallangarra. By the late 1880s, there was a growing consensus that a national government was needed to deal with issues such as trade, defence and immigration.

Convinced the colonies would be stronger if they united, Sir Henry Parkes, Premier of the Colony of New South Wales, gave a rousing address at Tenterfield, New South Wales in 1889 on the need for the Australian colonies to federate into one nation and calling for "a great national government for all Australians". The Tenterfield Oration, as it is now known, was significant because, although politicians had been discussing federation for some time, this was the first direct appeal to the public.

That great national government for all Australians, however, would be more than a decade in the making, as the various colonies quarrelled over provisions to protect their own self-interest, fearful that the colonies with the larger populations and industry, New South Wales and Victoria, would dominate the smaller colonies. Several plebiscites were held in all colonies until a form of consensus was reached, calling for a national convention to draft a constitution for a Commonwealth of Australia.

The Commonwealth of Australia Constitution Act 1900 (UK) was passed on 5th July 1900 and given Royal Assent by Queen Victoria on 9th July 1900. It was proclaimed on 1st January 1901 in Centennial Park, Sydney, and Sir Edmund Barton was sworn in as the interim Prime Minister, leading an interim Federal ministry of nine members.

The new constitution, as approved by Queen Victoria, established a bicameral Parliament, with a Senate and a House of Representatives, and a Governor-General as Queen Victoria's representative in Australia. Thus, on 1st January 1901, the six colonies became the Federated states of Australia, and Australia had become a nation — of sorts!

The important points to be taken from those words above is that the act declaring Australia to be a Federation of States was passed, not by the citizens of Australia, or even by parliaments elected by those Australians, but by the British Parliament, twelve thousand miles away and, in the main, by people who had never set foot in Australia. The act was ratified by Queen Victoria, and her representative in Australia, the Governor-General, was to be the de-facto Australian Head of State.

Yes, the parliament of the Commonwealth of Australia had some legislative powers, but in crucial matters it remained beholden to the parliament of the United Kingdom. The Australian Parliament, for example, did not hold the power to declare war — or peace for that matter — and should Britain decide to go to war, as would be the case on two occasions in the next half century, then Australia, by default, would also be at war.

1. https://historicalaustraliantowns.blogspot.com/2021/10/tingha-nsw-historic-tin-mining-town.html
2. *Armidale Express & New England General Advertiser*, 17 May 1873, p.6 (The name "Forties", seemingly, refers to a lawless gang who were terrorising the district at that time.)
3. Readers Digest Guide to Australian Places, Readers Digest, Sydney.

8
(1901 – 1914)

By the early 1900s the mining boom in Tingha was over. A few large mining companies moved into the area to mine the less accessible tin, but the days of individual miners scooping up surface tin with shovels were gone. Tingha's population dwindled to just a few hundred, fading away almost as quickly as it had appeared during the boom. The readily accessible surface and alluvial tin had run out, and most of the population did the same, as fast as they could.

In 1901 Johann Schoupp and his wife Catherine both died within a few months of each other in Tingha. Their two sons, Phillip Henry Schoupp and Phillip Joachim Schoupp, stayed on in Tingha and took jobs working for The Amalgamated Dredging Company at their Cope's Creek dredging site, two miles from Tingha.

On 15th March 1905, George James Woodbury, father of Aquilla and maternal grandfather of her son Solomon, died at the age of seventy-three years. He passed away peacefully at the *Soapworks* property of his son, Matthew, in Inverell. His funeral was one of the largest seen in Inverell to that time, and the *Inverell Times* carried an extensive eulogy.

Death of Mr. G. Woodbury.

We regret to record the death of Mr. George Woodbury, which occurred on Wednesday morning last at the residence of his son, Mr. M. W. Woodbury, Soapworks, Inverell. Deceased, who was 73 years of age, had been a sufferer from dropsy for a long time past, and during the last two months the ailment had grown worse and worse, ending in his death as stated. He was a pioneer farmer of the district. Some years ago, he joined the Salvation Army, and has ever since been a zealous member of that body, which, in view of the Army's rigid insistence of good living on the part of its members means a great deal. His death is greatly deplored, as he was held in high esteem by all who knew him. The late Mr. Woodbury leaves a widow and grown-up family, and a large circle of relatives and friends to mourn their sad loss.

The funeral took place on Thursday afternoon and was one of impressive dimensions, the vast concourse of mourning being a testimony to the respect in which deceased was held. It was conducted by the Salvation Army. The coffin was first taken to the Barracks where a stirring service was held, and afterwards the cortege left for the cemetery, the Army Band being at the head, and playing funeral music enroute. The sight was a sad one. At the cemetery fervent addresses were delivered by Adjutant Mayne and Bro. Morris, prayers were said, and hymns sang, including several of deceased's favourite hymns, viz., "Abide With Me" "We shall walk through the Valley," and others. [1]

In 1906, Solomon, the son of Phillip Henry Schoupp whom everyone called Henry to differentiate him from his brother who was also called Phillip, began working with his father and uncle at the Cope's Creek dredging site. But the work was unreliable because when the price of tin fell, The Amalgamated Dredging Company would temporarily close their operations purely to deny the supply of tin to the market and thus force the commodity price to rise again. It may have been good business practice for the company, but for its workers it meant times of hardship and deprivation.

In 1912, twenty-year-old Solomon Schoupp was visiting the Inverell Salvation Army, as was his practice from time to time.

"My name's Ella," the pretty young girl said in reply to his question. "Actually, it's Margaret, Margaret Ella Nerney, but everyone calls me Ella."

"I'm Solomon," he said. "Everyone calls me Solomon," he added with a smile, "or just Sol."

"Do you have 'the wisdom of Solomon' then?" she asked with a smile.

"Afraid not. My father's always telling me off for making bad decisions. Apparently, he has more wisdom than I do — or at least he thinks so."

Ella gave a smile that then turned into a cute laugh.

"So, Sol, what's your surname?"

"Schoupp," he replied. "I'm Solomon Schoupp."

"Shop," she repeated, using his pronunciation. "So, are you a storekeeper?"

Solomon laughed. He was beginning to realise how much he liked this Margaret whom everyone called Ella.

"No", he replied. "It sounds like 'Shop', but the spelling is S-C-H-O-U-P-P. We're miners."

"Wow! That's strange spelling. Sounds foreign, yet you don't have an accent."

"No," he said. "No accent, I hope. I was born in this country. My father came here as a young boy when his family immigrated from Germany."

Ella nodded.

"I've seen you here at the Salvation Army several times," she said, "but not regularly, not every week."

"We live in Tingha," Solomon replied. "My whole family are part of the Salvation Army in Tingha, but I like to come here to Inverell now and then. It's nice to be part of a bigger meeting, especially here in this nice new citadel. Our meeting place in Tingha is very small, of course."

The bandsmen were finding their places for the start of the meeting, and people were making their way towards their own seats.

"Are your parents here?" Solomon asked.

"Of course," she said, pointing to the band. "That's my father over there, manning the big drum."

"A-ha," Solomon said. "Now, if I were a regular member of this Corps, that big drum would be my job by tradition."

"Really?" Ella said, a little surprised. "I heard around here that the big drum was a Woodbury tradition."

"My mother was a Woodbury," Solomon told her. "Aquilla Woodbury, until she saw the light and married a Schoupp. So, I'm part of the Woodbury line."

They both laughed, and again Solomon thought how much he liked this girl.

"Do you mind if I sit with you during the meeting?" he asked.

"Well, I'll be sitting with my mother and the rest of my family," she replied, "but you're welcome to join us."

So it was that Solomon met the Nerney family, all nine of them

Ernest Thomas Nerney, he of the big drum fame, was, Ella's father and her mother's name was Mary Elizabeth Nerney. They had their seven children with them at the Inverell Salvation Army that night and Solomon found himself wedged in between Ella's mother on his left and Ella and the rest of the Nerney children on his right.[2]

Solomon also soon discovered that the first three Nerney children, Eva, Ted and Ella, had been born in Penrith, west of Sydney at the foot of the Blue Mountains. In 1895, the family had moved to Bingara for a short time, where their fourth child, Walter, was born in 1896 before the family moved to Inverell. The three youngest children, Olive, Ernest and Harry had all been born in Inverell.

"So, what brought your family from Penrith to Bingara and then Inverell, Mrs Nerney?" Solomon decided to ask after the meeting.

"Well, we were married at the Salvation Army in Penrith in 1888, but I'm originally from Bingara," Ella's mother replied. "And I guess I became a bit homesick. Do you know where Bingara is, Solomon?"

"Yes," Solomon replied. "It's about thirty miles west of here."

Mary Nerney nodded.

"Yes, though further than that by road, of course. I still have family there. I was Mary Brown before I married. I don't suppose you know of the Brown family in Bingara?"

"No, I'm afraid not," he replied. "I've never been to Bingara."

"No reason why you should have," she told him. "It's a very small place."

"Couldn't be any smaller than Tingha," Solomon said with a laugh, "although Tingha was a much bigger place when I was growing up. That was before the tin started to run out."

"Anyway," Mary Nerney continued, "it was hard for my husband to find work in Bingara, so we moved here in 1896, just after Walter was born.

Following that visit, Solomon's visits to the Inverell Salvation Army became much more frequent.

"You always seem to be going to Inverell for Army meetings," his mother said to him one weekend. "Isn't our small Corps here in Tingha good enough for you?"

"You know that's not right, Mother," he replied as he embraced her. "To be truthful, there's a young lady in Inverell I've become quite fond of."

Aquilla nodded knowingly as the pair broke their embrace.

"Yes", she said. "I thought it'd be that."

"He's a nice boy," Mary Nerney said to her daughter, Ella. "And he clearly has his eyes on you. But do you want to marry a miner? Mining has such an uncertain future."

Ella hesitated before answering.

"I'm not sure Mother," she said in the end. "I've thought about that, of course, and I'll think more about it too. Anyway, Solomon hasn't asked me to marry him yet."

There was also another reason Ella had been hesitant to answer her mother's question. She and Solomon had been surreptitiously spending quite a lot of time together — perhaps too much time. She was not totally sure but she thought she was probably pregnant. The next month would tell.

The pregnancy was confirmed a month later, and the humiliation of the predicament the young couple found themselves in began to consume their thinking. Had they been born a hundred years later, community sentiment about a pregnancy outside of marriage would probably not have raised an eyebrow, but in the early years of the 20th Century, attitudes were very different. Society, even that sector with little attachment to religious institutions and practices, placed great emphasis on the bonds of marriage. So, for two young people whose families were devout members of the Salvation Army, it was a catastrophe.

Solomon and Ella realised they were harbouring a shameful secret and, whilst they dreaded the prospect of doing so, they knew they had to share that secret with both Ella's parents in Inverell and Solomon's parents in Tingha. Solomon decided they should start in Tingha, believing they might receive a more sympathetic response from his parents than they expected from Ella's. It was a vain hope.

"What were you *thinking*?" his father asked, almost shouting.

"I guess we weren't thinking at all," Solomon replied, "we just ……got carried away. It only happened once."

"Well, once was obviously once too often. And you should have known that, Solomon."

"You'll have to be married immediately," Aquilla put in, "before the baby begins to show."

Ella and Solomon were holding hands below the table.

"We would have wanted to do that, anyway," Ella said.

"What have your parents had to say about this, Ella?" Phillip asked.

"They don't know about it yet, Mr Schoupp," she replied. "We're going to Inverell to tell them as soon as we leave here."

"Hmph!" Phillip said. "Well, good luck with that! I know your parents, Ella. They're good people, and you know the kind of reaction you'll get from them."

Ella's father, Ernest Nerney, spoke more quietly than Phillip Schoupp had spoken, but his words were no less severe. Despite their soft tone, they held a granitelike sense of accusation, and his quiet voice did not stop Mary Nerney from weeping.

"I'm ashamed of you, Ella," he said to his daughter. "You've been raised better than this. And you, young man," he said, turning to Solomon, "I don't know what to say to you. I thought you were a decent young man."

"He is a decent man, Father," Ella said defensively. "And we are very much in love."

Ernest Nerney released a long sigh.

"I'm very sorry, Sir," Solomon said to him.

"Sorry doesn't undo what's been done," Ella's father replied. "It shouldn't have happened, and you both know that."

"Well, it has happened, Father," Ella said quietly but firmly, "and we're both very sorry. But now we need to deal with it."

"We do indeed," Ernest Nerney said. "You will be married immediately, but not here in Inverell. You'll be married in Tingha. It's a smaller community and a smaller Salvation Army Corps."

The implication was clear — the fewer people who knew about this calamity the better, and marrying in Tingha would reduce the degree of shame and community condemnation on the family.

"Once the baby begins to show," he continued, "you will cease visiting us here in Inverell, and, after the baby's born, you will not return here until I give my permission. Is that clear?"

Ella and Solomon both nodded their assent before Ernest Nerney stood and left the room. Mary Nerney looked at her daughter, longing to embrace her and to give her some acknowledgement of motherly love. After a few moments she decided not to do so, and followed her husband from the room.

Margaret Ella Nerney married Solomon James Schoupp at the Tingha Salvation Army on 5th November 1914, and the couple immediately moved in with Solomon's parents in Tingha. It was only two days after the marriage, however, that Phillip sat his son down for a serious chat.

"You need to move away from Tingha, Sol," he said to his son as they sat at the kitchen table with cups of tea. "Both you, and your wife. There are three good reasons, not all to do with the baby."

Solomon looked at his father in silence, waiting for him to continue.

"The first reason is the irregular work here in the mine. You've got a wife to provide for, and a child on the way. And, I daresay, in time, there'll be more children. Work with the dredging company is far too unreliable for a family man."

Solomon did not want to leave his family in Tingha but he did not say anything at that point.

"The second reason," Phillip continued, "does concern the baby. People around here might be simple folk, Sol, but they can count to nine! If you stay here, as soon as the baby begins to show, you and your wife will be shamed and condemned by the community, even by some of those who are part of the Salvation Army here. Your mother and I will be made to share in that shame and condemnation, and I will not allow that to happen to Aquilla."

"And the third reason?" Solomon asked.

"We're in a war now, Sol," he said. "Britain's been drawn into the conflict in Europe, simply because some young Serbian fool assassinated the Austro-Hungarian heir."

Solomon knew about the war — everyone did. The local newspapers had been reporting about it for three months. In 1914, the European powers were divided into two opposing alliances, the Triple Entente, consisting of France, Russia and Britain, and the Triple Alliance, made up of Germany, Austria-Hungary and Italy. Tensions in the Balkans had come to a head on 28th June that year, following the assassination of Archduke Franz Ferdinand, the Austro-Hungarian heir, by Gavrilo Princip, a Bosnian Serb. Austria-Hungary blamed Serbia, and the interlocking alliances involved the nations of Europe in a series of increasingly tense diplomatic exchanges. On 28th July 1914, Austria-Hungary had declared war on Serbia. Russia came to Serbia's defence and, by early August, the conflict had expanded to include Germany, France, and Britain, along with their respective colonial empires, including Australia.

"The British army is about to find itself fighting in France against the Fatherland, Germany. That means Australia, too will be at war with Germany," Johann continued. "If that happens — and I think it's almost unavoidable — it's going to make things very difficult for those of us with a German heritage."

"How so?" Solomon asked.

"There's no telling how bad it might get," his father replied. "Who knows? We might even be interned in camps as enemy aliens. At the very least we'll be ostracised by the local population."

"Surely not!" Solomon exclaimed. "People know us here! They know we are patriotic Australians."

Phillip eyed his son over the rim of his tea cup.

"They know we have German blood, Sol, and that'll be enough. I think it wise that you take your young wife and move away from Tingha."

"To Inverell?" Solomon asked, but his father shook his head.

"No, Inverell wouldn't work for you even if Ella's parents would allow it, which they won't. You are as well known in Inverell as you are here. Go someplace where you aren't known. Start again. Even change your name if you think it wise."

Solomon recoilled at the thought of having to change his name. He resolved in his own mind never do that.

"Armidale?" he asked.

"Yes," his father said. "Armidale would probably work. Glen Innes might be better."

"We don't know a soul in Glen Innes," Solomon retorted.

"Then Glen Innes is the place for you," his father said.

On 10th November 1914, Solomon and Ella waved a sad goodbye to their family in Tingha, then called at Inverell to say their tearful farewells to Ella's family, before making their way to Glen Innes, forty miles east of Inverell. They travelled from Inverell to Glen Innes by bus, with Ella weeping for most of the two hour journey. In Glen Innes they alighted from the bus in front of the Town Hall and wondered how they were going to find a cheap hotel or boarding house in this town about which they knew absolutely nothing. It was there on the footpath that Ella drew Solomon's attention to a notice attached to the front door of the Town Hall.

> *Available of immediate rent: two bedroom,*
> *council cottage in Grey Street. Apply within.*

Ella remained on the footpath with their luggage whilst Solomon went into the Town Hall to enquire. Fifteen minutes later he emerged with a smile on his face.

"Did we get it," Ella asked.

"We not only got the cottage," Solomon replied, "I got a job, too. They were looking for a truck driver to work with the road maintenance gang for the Municipal Council. I start tomorrow."

1. *Inverell Times*, 18 March 1905, p.2
2. Eveline Eliizabeth Nernery (always known as Eva) was born on 22nd August 1889; Edward George Nernery (known as Ted) was born on 10th February 1891; Margaret Ella Nernery (always known as Ella) was born on 9th March 1893; Walter John Nernery was born on 6th August 1896; Olive Ruth Nernery was born on 5th June 1898; Ernest Winborne Nernery was born on 17th January 1901; William Henry Nernery, the baby, (always known as Harry) had been born on 17th August 1910.

9
(1914 – 1919)

Glen Innes, like the rest of Australia, was gripped with nationalist, patriotic fervour. This manifested itself in a sense of excitement, especially among young men who, in the main, answered the call to war with a sense of adventure, duty and enthusiasm. Quickly, the Australian armed forces grew from 3,000 to over 50,000 as young men enlisted, keen to be part of the big adventure which they thought would soon be over. That sense of excitement and enthusiasm generated a society in which acceptance of war duties was expected and celebrated, whereas refusal or reluctance to enlist was met with accusations of treason and cowardice.

Local communiy leaders, themselves too old to go to war, made their sentiments very clear — it was the duty of evey able-bodied young man to enlist for overseas duty in the service of the Motherland, England. Politicians, church leaders, newspaper editors and industry spokesmen spoke out constantly in support of the war and urged all men of military age to enlist. Just why the Motherland had become engaged in this conflict on the European continent was not widely understood, however. Indeed, most gave the question little thought.

The editorials in the local newspaper, the *Glen Innes Examiner,* called on all Australians to support the war effort and for all able-bodied men of military age to enlist in the great cause of defending the Motherland against perceived German aggression. Community attitudes towards eligible men who had not enlisted quickly hardened and the *Examiner* was not backward in declaring such men to be undeserving shirkers, slackers and perhaps even cowards.

The Australian government, as in England, quite unashamedly weaponised the influence of women, including wives, as a strategy targeting manhood, intended to drive men to enlist because of a perceived blow to their own sexuality and gender identity. White feathers had become a symbol of cowardice and a woman publicly confronting a man, handing him one and asking why he had not enlisted effectively told him he was not a "real man" and that his apparent lack of masculinity disgusted women. Solomon had his reasons for not enlisting, but he was finding it increasingly difficult to avoid probing questions from his neighbours, from workmates and even from strangers in the street.

When shopping in the main street of Glen Innes one Saturday morning, Solomon was approached by an attractive woman who placed a white feather on his lapel, looked at him with disdain, then turned on her heels and walked away. It wasn't the last time it would happen to him, and, on occasions, women would stop him in the street and ask why he had not enlisted. His stock answer to those questions was simply to say, "You wouldn't understand, ma'am," and then to walk away, often with the woman calling after him, "Coward!".

Whilst Solomon had determined not to change his German surname, for a time at least he was able to avoid scrutiny of his genealogical background because the way his name was pronounced. Schoupp pronounced "Shop", was not instantly recognisable as being German. People may have thought "Shop" was an unusual name but, in the early days of the war at least, few associated it with German heritage and Solomon and Ella learned to modify their signatures, making the spelling of the name all but illegible.

There were occasions however, when giving the correct spelling of the name was unavoidable and, in a small town such as Glen Innes word soon spread that the "Shop" family were of German extraction.

"Perhaps we should've moved to a bigger place, Sol," Ella said to her husband one night. "Maybe somewhere like Sydney where fewer people would know us."

"We can't keep running away from who we are, and what we are, Ell'," Solomon replied. "I'm still resentful of the fact that we had to move away from Tingha because of a mistake we made. We're going to have to weather this storm and manage it as best we can."

Ella sighed deeply and began to weep.

"I hate this, Sol," she said between tears. "I hate it when people in the street call me a traitor. Yesterday, one woman shouted at me 'You should be locked up!'"

Solomon put his arm around his wife to comfort her.

"We'll get through this, Ell'," he said. "This'll pass. People are saying this war can't last long."

At work, too, Solomon found himself confronted with awkward questions about his hesitancy to join up. Most of the young men who had been part of the road maintenance gang had enlisted, leaving Solomon as the youngest in the gang.

"All the young men on the road gang have gone off to enlist, Sol. Apart from you, that is," said Arthur Sutton, foreman of Solomon's work group. "I guess you'll be going off soon too?"

"Perhaps, but not yet. Not for a while," Solomon replied noncommittally.

"What's holding you back, Sol? You don't strike me as a coward."

"I'm not a coward, Arthur," Solomon replied, defensively, "but I've got my reasons. You wouldn't understand."

"Well, you need to know, people are talking about you, Sol. Many think you should've already joined up."

Solomon nodded.

"I know that Arthur," he said. "I've even had women give me white feathers in the street. It's just something I have to live with at the moment while I work through it. Like I said, most people wouldn't understand my situation, and it's impossible for me to explain my reasons."

The fact was that the war, and Australia's response to it, constituted a huge dilemma for Solomon. He was patriotic, he loved the country of his birth and he was no coward. Yet, for him, the call to arms meant pointing a rifle at his own family.

"How could I be sure, Ell'," he asked his wife, "that the man I point my rifle at, the man I might shoot, isn't my cousin, or an uncle? I don't think I could do that."

The couple sat in silence, unable to find a way forward. Then Solomon spoke again.

"There's also the pregnancy to think about, Ell'. The babe will arrive sometime in June next year."

"If you have to go, Sol, then I can manage the birth of our child," Ella replied with tears in her eyes. "I really don't want you to go — I can't stand the thought of losing you. But I don't think the baby is the main factor in your decision about whether to go or not. Mother would come from Inverell to help me. My parents are still angry and ashamed of me, but Mother wouldn't let me go through the birth of our child alone. I know that. The real issue is your German blood, your German heritage, and I fully understand that dilemma. I don't think there's a way around that. You may have to sit out this war, and the local community is going to make that very difficult for you — for both of us."

As the next few months passed, community attitudes hardened into intolerance towards people of German, Austrian and Hungarian descent, and Solomon remembered how his father had warned him of this. In the Australian census of 1911, around 36,000 people had identified themselves as having been born in Germany or Austria-Hungary. Then, in late 1914, those of German descent were required to register their details with the nearest police station. Some citizens of Austro-German descent tried to reaffirm their loyalty to Australia by enlisting to serve in the

AIF. Others changed their names, something Solomon had promised himself he would not do.

The predictions of Solomon's father in Tingha, about the possibility of internment camps for those of German descent also became a reality when, under the War Precautions Act of 1914, the Australian Government established several camps in which almost 7,000 people were interned for the duration of the war. The Schoupp family, in Tingha and in Glen Innes, were not interned but Solomon's father, along with thousands of others of German descent, lived under a system of parole throughout the war.

On 26th April 1915 media releases informed the Australian people that at dawn on the previous day, 25th April, Australian and New Zealand troops, which they called the ANZACs, had landed on the Gallipoli Peninsula, adjacent to the Dardanelles and were fighting against Turkish defenders. Initial reports gave little detail.

DECISIVE ACTION.
THE FIGHT FOR THE DARDANELLES.
UNOFFICIAL GREEK REPORT.

ATHENS, Saturday.
Unofficial reports are that a decisive action at the Dardanelles has begun. The Allied squadrons bombarded the Straits at various points west of Gallipoli, and a landing has been effected at three points – Cape Suvla and Bulair, Gallipoli Peninsula, and Enos (at the mouth of the Maritza, near Dedeagatch).[2]

By 28th April, although the Australian public did not realise it at the time, media releases were already being sanitised and flavoured for public consumption. The media release on that day, under the heading of *"Successful Land Operations"*, described the action at Gallipoli as *"a magnificent achievement"* where Allied troops had *"won distinction"* through their *"splendid gallantry"*³ They had indeed fought gallantly, but they had been thrown into a poorly conceived and poorly executed campaign which, notwithstanding the courage and valour of the troops, could not have been won.

On 29th April, the Australian Prime Minister, Andrew Fisher, announced in the House of Representatives that a cablegram had been received from the Secretary of State for the Colonies, dated London, 27th April. The cablegram stated:

> *His Majesty's Government desire me to offer you the warmest congratulations on the splendid gallantry and magnificent achievements of your contingent in the successful progress of operations at the Dardanelles.*

The Governor General sent a cablegram in reply:

> *The Government and people of Australia are deeply gratified to learn that their troops have won distinction in their first encounter with the enemy. We are confident that they will carry the King's colours to further victory.* ⁴

Fisher's reading of the two cablegrams in parliament was met with loud cheers from both sides of the House.

In Glen Innes, unaware of the military defeat that was unfolding on the shores of Gallipoli, twenty-two-year-old Solomon read the encouraging news of the Gallipoli campaign to his wife, Ella.

"If I'd know they were sending our troops to Gallipoli to fight the Turks, Ell', I would've enlisted," he said. "I thought they'd be sent to France to fight the Germans, my father's people."

Solomon's presence at Gallipoli, had he gone, would have made little if any difference to the outcome of the campaign. The ANZAC troops had landed on an area of narrow beach beyond which was steep, rugged terrain. Once on the beach, many units had become separated from one another as they began moving up the tangle of complex spurs and ravines in the semi-darkness. Turkish resistance was strong, and the ANZACs were subjected to devastating rifle fire, machine gun fire, and artillery bombardments. By the end of the first day, the ANZAC troops were forced to dig in, having lost 2,000 men without securing their high-ground objectives. For the next eight months, the ANZACs would fight gallantly to hold their trench positions on the rugged ridges above the beach and, despite their bravery, they would advance little further than the positions they had taken on the first day of the landings. An indication of the gallantry of the ANZAC forces is seen in the fact that a total of nine Victoria Crosses were awarded to Australians during the Gallipoli campaign. More than 8,700 Australians and 2,770 New Zealanders were killed during the campaign, almost fifteen percent of those who had landed on the peninsula. Despite the Gallipoli campaign being a military defeat, it is widely considered to be the beginning of Australian and New Zealand national consciousness.

The one positive consequence of the war for Solomon was the availability of work in Glen Innes. With so many young men enlisting in the AIF, there were plenty of job vacancies, so Solomon was able to find some extra weekend work which supplemented the rather low salary he was being paid as part of the road maintenance gang.

On 15th July 1915, Solomon and Ella welcomed their first child, a healthy daughter whom they named Phyllis Jean.

It was in late January 1916, as Solomon was walking through the main street of Glen Innes, Grey Street, on his way to work that he was confronted by an AIF sergeant at a recruiting station in front of the Town Hall.

"'ere t' sign up are y', mate?" the sergeant called to him as he walked by. Solomon shook his head and continued walking.

"What are y' then?" the sergeant called out. "A conchie or a coward?"

That stopped Solomon in his tracks, and he turned to confront the sergeant.

"I'm not a conscientious objector," he said, "and I'm no coward. I love this country and I'm a patriotic citizen."

"Then, y' should be signing up. Any patriotic man would! What's stopping y'?"

"You wouldn't understand," Solomon replied as he prepared to walk off, but stopped when he heard another voice behind him.

"Perhaps I'll understand."

Solomon turned around to see a recruiting officer, a lieutenant, perhaps in his mid-twenties, with ruffled sandy hair and the trace of a welcoming smile on his face — though whether the smile was genuine or merely part of his strategy to entice men to enlist, was unclear.

"It's okay, Sergeant," the officer said. "I'll handle this one."

"Lieutenant Watson," the officer said by way of introduction, as he reached out and shook hands with Solomon. "What's your story, boy?"

"I'm not a boy," Solomon responded. "I'm twenty-three years old, a married man with a young child."

"All the more reason why you should be signing up," Lieutenant Watson countered. "The Motherland needs men like you."

Strange that he talks about England as the Motherland, Solomon thought. *My father talks about Germany as the Fatherland, yet we're all Australians.* But he kept these thoughts to himself.

Yet, for reasons he could not explain, he felt a certain rapport with this Lieutenant Watson. Perhaps this man might understand the conundrum he faced. So he opened up about his family name, Schoupp, explained its origins and his family background which prevented him from signing up.

"It'd be like going to war against my own family," he said. "Do you understand that, Lieutenant?"

Watson stood there nodding, then reached out to put a hand on Solomon's shoulder in a sign of friendship and acceptance, genuine or otherwise.

"I do, Sol," he said. "That's a huge dilemma."

For a few moments the two men stood there saying nothing, Solomon with tears beginning to form in his eyes. Unlike the Sergeant who had first accosted Solomon in the street, Lieutenant Watson had been well trained in recruitment techniques. He knew when to remain silent and to let a man think about his debt to his country. "Use silence as a weapon," he'd been taught. "When you see a man is on the brink of committing to the cause, let him think, let the emotions build, watch the eyes and know just when to put voice to the challenge again."

Eventually, the Lieutenant spoke to Solomon again.

"What would you say if I told you there's a way you could sign up and serve your country without taking up arms against the Germans?" he asked. "A way that you could actually save lives, rather than take lives?"

Solomon stood there silently, waiting for Watson to continue.

"I could sign you up as a stretcher-bearer," he said. "You'd be carrying our wounded soldiers back to aid-stations behind the lines, getting them to places where they'd have life-saving treatment."

"I'd be in uniform?" Solomon asked.

"Of course. You'd be an important part of the army."

"And I wouldn't be expected to shoot at Germans?"

The officer shook his head.

"Stretcher-bearers are unarmed," he said, "They're not even trained to use weapons."

Solomon stood there silently, trying to take in the role that was being offered to him.

"I won't lie to you, Sol," Watson continued. "It's a dangerous job. Part of the time you'd be carrying wounded behind our trenches back to the aid-stations, but at other times, you'd be expected to go out into no-man's-land, between our trenches and those of the enemy, to retrieve our fallen soldiers. You'd be going out there with nothing to protect yourself other than your steel helmet and the red and white armband with SB on it. Some of the enemy would respect that armband, provided it was clearly visible and not covered in mud. But ohers wouldn't, and would fire on you."

"So it sounds like stretcher-bearers have a short life expectancy at the front?" Solomon said, more as a statement than a question.

Watson nodded.

"Like I said, Sol, it's a dangerous job. There'll be times of unrelenting boredom, mixed with times of utter terror."

"I'll need to talk to my wife about it," Solomon said as he prepared to leave.

"You know where to find us, Sol," Watson replied as he turned and walked away, not expecting he would ever see the young man again.

The discussion with Ella that night took several hours and, even at the end of it, the couple had reached no decision. The next morning, Solomon retreated to spend time alone with his deliberations before going back to the house to speak with Ella.

"I think I need to do this, Ell'," he said. "It's my patriotic duty to our country and it's a way to serve without taking up arms against my father's people."

Ella nodded.

"There was another white feather in our mail box this morning," she said.

"I can live with the white feathers, Ell'," Solomon replied, "and I can ignore the comments about being a conscientious objector or a coward. What I can't ignore is the knowledge gnawing away within me that this country has been good to me, to us. We owe a lot to this country. I think I have to answer the opportunity that's been given to me to serve."

Three days later, on 2nd February 1916, and after further discussions with Ella, Solomon returned to the recruiting station in front of the Town Hall.

"I'm looking for Lieutenant Watson," he told a sergeant, not the same sergeant who had first confronted him about signing up.

Lieutenant Watson, when he was found, was more than a little surprised to see that the young man to whom he had spoken about being a stretcher-bearer had returned. He was unsure at first whether Solomon had returned to enlist or whether he was just being courteous enough to return to tell him he had decided not to.

"I'm not sure I expected to see you again, Sol," he said. "What have you decided?"

"I'm here to join up as a stretcher-bearer," Solomon said. "It's a way that I can do my duty."

Within an hour, Solomon was a member of the AIF — Private Solomon James Schoupp, service number 1253, stretcher-bearer with the 33rd Batallion AIF. He was told to go home to await his call-up orders.

It was several days before these came, hand delivered by a sergeant from the recruitment station. They instructed him to be at the Town Hall recruitment station at 0800hrs on Monday 14th February 1916, with minimal luggage. Ella accompanyied him to the Town Hall and they shared a long embrace before Solomon had to board a bus bound for Armidale.

"Come back to me, Sol," she said, wiping the tears from her cheeks.

"I'll be back. And I'll write when I can," he replied before a final embrace and kiss.

The newly enlisted men alighted from the bus in Armidale in heavy rain and in the midst of a large encampment of tents. Immediately, they were assailed by orders being shouted at them in military fashion.

"Over there! Get in line — a straight line you miserable lot! God knows how we're gonna defeat the Huns with the likes of you! Get your hands out of your pockets, soldier. You're in the army now!"

Three days later, Solomon wrote his first letter to his wife, Ella. It took more than ten days to be delivered to her, only sixty miles away, and parts of it had been redacted by the military censors.

18 February 1916

My dear Ella, and baby Phyllis.

Well, we are camped at the Armidale show grounds. It's a huge camp, tents as far as you can see. I've no idea how many men are here but there's a lot. Tommy McArdle from Tingha is here. Do you remember Tommy? His father, "Old Tom", owns the grocery store in Ruby Street. Seems all the men here are from the areas around ▓▓▓▓▓▓▓▓▓▓▓▓▓▓ *and some from a bit further north. So this batallion, the 33rd, is being called "New England's Own." Most of the men are being given rifle training, but my training is restricted to carrying soldiers around on stretchers. (They have to pretend to be wounded — they're even ordered to groan, as if wounded). I'm also being given some basic first-aid training. Fortunately, they do the first-aid training in tents – it hasn't stopped raining since we arrived here.*

I've no idea how long we'll be here. Some are saying ▓▓▓▓ *and some say longer. I hear we'll eventually be taken to Sydney by train and from there we'll be shipped off to the war. Again, I have no idea where — some are saying we'll be sent to ▮▮▮▮, others are saying ▮▮▮▮ In truth, nobody really knows.*

Give little Phyllis a big hug from me and keep my picture close by so she'll know who I am when I return. Try not to worry. I love you both very much and will write again when I can.

Sol

1. *The Inverell Times*, Sat 18 Mar 1905, p.2
2. *The Brisbane Courier*, 26th April 1915, p.7
3. *The Brisbane Courier*, 28th April 1915, p.7
4. *The Brisbane Courier*, 30th April 1915, p.7

10
(1916 – 1919)

Two months of training continued at Armidale — rifle training and bayonet training for most, first-aid training for Solomon and a few other stretcher-bearers, all of whom were conscientious objectors prepared to serve but not to fight. And for all, endless marching.

"Seems like they think we're going to march all the way to Germany," Solomon said jokingly to his mate Tommy McArdle. "Why else would we need so much marching practice?"

All were kitted out with khaki uniforms, steel helmets, gas masks and, for the stretcher-bearers, the red and white armbands Lieutenant Watson had told Solomon would be his only protection in no-man's-land.

"This is your introduction to army life. It's where you'll learn to be a soldier," a sergeant-major bellowed at them. "You'll learn how to work as a member of a team to accomplish tasks. Take it in! Learn it well! Your life will depend on it."

Every morning commenced, before dawn, with physical fitness exercises and then, after breakfast, long runs with heavy backpacks, learning how to march and follow commands, military discipline and command structure and, for most, how to use their weapons. Most soldiers were issued with a .303 rifle with bayonet attachment. A small number, seemingly chosen at random, were trained to use the heavy Vickers machine guns. Solomon was paired with another stretcher-bearer and spent many hours running around the encampment with a stretcher loaded with bags of sand.

Sandbagged trenches had been dug to simulate trench warefare and to train the troops in defending their trenches, and attacking enemy ones. In places, the trenches were equipped with wooden periscopes, allowing some of the soldiers to look across no-man's-land towards the enemy trenches. All took their turn at looking through the periscopes.

The large number of troops at the Armidale show ground were divided into different Companies, and on any given day these Companies could be seen undergoing different training. Some might be learning how to keep their rifle clean and combat ready, some might be listening to instructions from the Medical Officer on things like how to prevent sore feet (basically, keep your socks dry!). Some might be practising donning gas masks on the call of "GAS!", whilst others completed endless hours of marching. Some might be learning to defend, their trench line as others charged across no-man's land, screaming and with bayonets at the ready, in a mock attack. The "attacking troops" were under strict orders not to stop to assist any fallen comrades. That was the job of the stretcher-bearers who followed close behind the attacking troops, charged with retrieving those who had been ordered to "fall wounded" during the mock attack.

March 1916 was a wet month in Armidale and the mock battlefields and trenches of the showground quickly became churned up and ankle deep in mud. The soldiers cursed it, not realising the battlefields of Europe would be far worse.

The mock attacks, with blank ammunition, were as close as they could get to simulating real trench warfare and, after more than two months of training, most of the troops were becoming restless. They itched to get to the real war, believing they were ready to face the Germans. They were not.

The 33rd Battalion AIF was eventually moved to Armidale railway station in groups, over three days, 28th – 30th April 1916, and boarded troop trains that would take them to Sydney. From Central Station, the troops were taken by trucks and buses to Woolloomooloo Finger Wharf, to the troop transport *HMAT Marathon* which was docked there. Solomon Schoupp and Tommy McArdle from Tingha had become close friends during training at Armidale and slung their hammocks next to each other on the second deck of *Marathon*. Neither knew, of course, that Private Thomas (Tommy) McArdle would be killed in action at Villers-Bretonneux, France, on 4th April 1918, or that Private Solomon Schoupp, stretcher-bearer with the 33rd Battalion, would retrieve the body of his twenty-two-year-old friend from no-man's-land.

HMAT Marathon sailed from Sydney on the morning of 4th May 1916 with orders to disembark the troops at Cairo, Egypt. Enroute, however, those orders were rescinded, and *Marathon* sailed directly to the United Kingdom, with ports of call in Albany Western Australia, Durban, Cape Town, and Dakar, before arriving at Southampton on 9th July 1916.

One week later, in Tingha, Solomon's father, Phillip Henry Schoupp, died suddenly of a heart attack on 16th July 1916. Ella wrote to Solomon, informing him of the loss of his father, but it was three months before the letter reached him, by which time he was undergoing further training in England. In her letter, Ella included a cutting from a Tingha newspaper.

> ### *Death of an Old Resident.*
> *One of the old identities of Tingha crossed the Great Divide on Saturday last. We refer to Mr Phillip Schoupp, who breathed his last in the Tingha Cottage Hospital. The deceased, who had more than reached the allotted three score and ten (being 79 years of age) was always known as a kind husband and fond father. The funeral took place on Sunday afternoon, the band of the Salvation Army preceding the cortege, while the officers conducted the burial service. The late Mr Schoupp is survived by a widow, and the following children :– Mesdames John and Alfred Cox, Tingha ; Mrs Alf Cooper, Tingha ; Mrs Windren, Victoria ; Mr George Shoupp, while another son, Mr S. J. Schoupp, is at present on active service. To these the utmost sympathy is felt in, their sad loss.* [1]

Ella also wrote to her mother-in-law, Aquilla, in Tingha and expressed her "deep sorrow" at the passing of her father-in-law whom she said, had always been a kind man to her "even when I least deserved it." She explained in her letter the reason she would not attend the funeral in Tingha.

> *I respect the wishes of your late husband that I do not return to Tingha whilst Phyllis is so young because there are those in the community who might direct shame and condemnation on you at this very sad time. But I find solace in the knowledge that you have your four loving*

daughters and your son George, in Tingha to support you. You are constantly in my prayers.

Ernest and Mary Nerney, and many others from the Inverell Salvation Army, did attend Phillip's funeral in Tingha.

In England, immediately after disembarking at Southampton, the 33rd Battalion was moved to Larkhill, on Salisbury Plain in the shadows of Stonehenge and there they underwent five months of intense training under British officers and NCOs to prepare them for the rigours of trench warfare on the Western Front. Solomon wrote to Ella regularly, though the letters took months to arrive, telling her he was well and that the battalion was undergoing training in England. He also wrote to her about "the amazing stones of Stonehenge", but those details were redacted by the censors who did not want the locations of any troops revealed.

The 33rd Battalion became part of the 9th Brigade of the 3rd Australian Division and crossed the English Channel on the ferry *Mona Queen* in late November 1916, disembarking onto French soil at the port of Le Havre in the Normandy region of north-western France. From Le Havre, the battalion was transported by train to Bailleul, a small town located in French Flanders, less than two miles from the Belgian border and sixteen miles northwest of Lille. At Bailleul the marching commenced. The battalion headed to the Front and occupied a section of front-line trenches around Armentières.

The line at Armentières was a quiet sector, referred to by the British as a "nursery sector"' although the battle-scarred landscape, both forward of the trenches and behind them, bore testimony to the fact that it had not always been so. Not a single tree was standing and the land all around showed evidence of heavy shelling from both sides. The Battle of Armentières, which some called the Battle of Lille, had been fought by German and Franco-British forces in the area in October 1914 as both sides sought to outflank each other in a campaign that had been called "The Race to the Sea". Neither side had won the race and, by the time of the AIF 33rd Battalion's arrival, a quiet but uneasy stalemate had settled on the battlefield. Many hours were spent peering through the trench periscopes at the enemy trenches some two hundred yards away across no-man's-land, but hostilities were restricted to the occasional sniper shot from both sides. Stretcher-bearers were given priority access to the periscopes and charged with familiarising themselves with no-man's-land so that they would be ready for action when they heard the call – *"Stretcher-bearers!".*

Living in the trenches with the rest of the battalion, Solomon experienced no animosity or even friction from the other soldiers because of his decision not to take up arms. Though the battalion had not yet been involved in heavy fighting, the armed men realised, it seemed, that the time would come when their lives might well depend upon the stretcher-bearers. Throughout December 1916, the troops of the AIF 33rd rotated between occupying the forward trenches and undertaking training behind the forward trenches, as they became accustomed to life on the battlefield of the Western Front. Then immediately after Christmas 1916, the 33rd Battalion began launching raids against the German positions. They faced staunch and resolute resistance, including heavy machine gun fire, and Solomon, for the first time, found himself retrieving fallen comrades and helping to carry them to aid-stations behind their own trenches. Initially, Solomon and his stretcher-bearing partner sought shelter in the large shell holes in no-man's land, but they quickly learned that climbing out of those muddy holes with a loaded stretcher was all but impossible. Thereafter, they avoided them and ran straight for their own trenches across open ground, carrying fallen comrades who were often just dropped unceremoniously into the relative safety of their own trenches.

Solomon wrote regularly to Ella, and occasionally to his mother in Tingha, not knowing when or if his letters would reach them. Realising that censors would remove any mention of places or of actions, his letters became little more than short notes, scribbled in pencil in the muddy trenches and informing his loved ones he was safe and well, even when he was not.

The 33rd Battalion's first major battle came in mid-1917 when the British shifted the focus of the Allied operations to the Ypres sector in Belgium. Along with the rest of the 9th Brigade, the 33rd Battalion led the 3rd Division's assault on Messines which was launched on 7th June 1917. The battle began with the detonation of nineteen huge mines in tunnels which had been dug beneath the German front line and, immediately after the detonation of the mines, the 33rd Battalion went over the sandbags to charge what was left of the German trenches. The 33rd suffered two hundred casualties before they even got out of their own trenches due to Allied gas-shells that had dropped short and fallen on their own trenches instead of on those of the enemy. Nevertheless, the battalion went over the top at the appointed hour and secured their objective in the enemy trenches. However, they were able to hold the ground they had gained for only two days before being forced back to their own trenches by intense and constant German artillery bombardment. The battalion's casualties during that battle amounted to ninety-two killed in action and two hundred and sixty wounded — the heaviest casualties they would suffer for the entire war.

One of those injured during the retreat on 9th June 1917, was stretcher-bearer Private Solomon Schoupp who was hit in the thigh by sniper fire as he endeavoured to carry a wounded comrade to safety. He himself was carried to the field hospital for treatment. Fortunately, the bullet had missed bones and vital arteries and, after treatment and recuperation, he re-joined his battalion on 13th July 1917. Due to nerve damage in his leg, however, he would walk with a limp for the rest of his life. He did not write to inform Ella or his parents that he had been wounded.

After the battle of Messines, the battalion was engaged in actions during the Third Battle of Ypres in October 1917. Moving up to Zonnebeke on the night of 2nd October, in the first week of the push against Broodseinde, the battalion was assigned a support role in the battle, partly because their numbers were still depleted following the battle of Messines and partly because the narrowness of the front at Broodseinde limited the role of the 3rd Division.

Then came Passchendaele, perhaps remembered as a symbol of one of the worst horrors of the First World War — the constant rain, the mud, the madness and the senseless slaughter of hundreds of thousands of men on the Western Front. The sheer futility of the fighting and the reckless disregard by some of the war's senior leaders, officers such as Field Marshal Sir Douglas Haig, for the lives of men under their command was scandalous and would remain controversial long after the war. Haig commanded the British and Allied Army to arguably some of its greatest victories, but he also insisted on pressing on with campaigns and sacrificing men under his command when success was clearly impossible. Passchendaele was such a case.

Commencing on 12th October 1917, the Australian 3rd Division, including the 33rd Battalion, was thrown into the assault during the First Battle of Passchendaele, together with troops from Britain, New Zealand and Canada. Constant heavy rain and artillery bombardment had reduced the Passchendaele battlefield to a quagmire where the troops simply ground themselves into the mud, unable to move forward and often unable to move backward as well. Hundreds of thousands of soldiers on opposing sides, knee-deep in mud, blood and gore, attempted to attack and counterattack across an open, colourless landscape devoid of buildings, trees or natural cover. Conditions for the soldiers were absolutely appalling. The mud virtually made rifles impossible to fire, it prevented artillery from being moved from place to place and it slowed the stretcher-bearers to a virtual crawl, sometimes to a literal crawl, as they tried to carry loaded stretchers through thigh-deep mud. With the constant rain, the trenches filled with water, mud and blood, and some soldiers drowned. Haig had pledged that he would not commit the country to heavy losses. Yet the armies under his command suffered some 275,000 casualties at Passchendaele, including 38,000 Australian dead, 5,300 New Zealanders and more than 15,600 Canadians. For five months, the 33rd alternated between front line service and short periods of rest and training behind their lines. At the end, the point of it all was unclear. In 1918, all the ground gained at Passchendaele by the Allies was evacuated in the face of a looming German offensive.

It was at Passchendaele that Solomon Schoupp began to question the purpose of war. He remained patriotic, loyal and obedient to orders, but his attitude and sentiments were changing. His letters to Ella began to change too. For the first time they talked about the horror of the war rather than just reassurances that he was well. From Passchendaele he wrote:

> *I think I will never understand why our national leaders send their young men off to fight and to die in futile wars. Perhaps those national leaders on both sides should come here to* ▓▓▓▓▓▓▓▓. *It is hell on earth.*

It was also at Passchendaele that Solomon first became ill with pneumonia which, until the end of the war, caused him to be periodically hospitalised. He would spend short times in field hospitals, but those times of treatment and recovery were far too short because stretcher-bearers were urgently needed on the front line. Between periods of hospitalisation, he would return to serve with the battalion, but he never truly recovered from the pneumonia.

In March 1918, the Germans launched a major offensive and the 33rd Battalion was rushed to the line in front of the vital railhead at Amiens. There, the 33rd were engaged in heavy fighting and led a counterattack at Hangard Wood on 20th March. On 4th April, the battalion helped defeat a major German drive on Villers-Bretonneux. A few days after the battle at Villers-Bretonneux, Solomon sat in the trench to write two short but melancholy letters — one to his wife and one to his mother.

He wrote to Ella.

> *My heart aches today. Tommy McArdle from Tingha was killed in action the day before yesterday, 4th April. I thought the death and suffering that surrounds us here had made me immune to these feelings, but I have been hit hard by Tommy's death. He was a good mate. They took his body for burial well behind our lines. . . .*

He wrote a similar letter to his mother, Aquilla, in Tingha, but added a personal request.

> *I would appreciate it if you would go and give my condolences to Tommy's parents. Please tell old Tom that I saw his boy fall and that he did not suffer. Actually, that's not true. I didn't see Tommy fall but I think that, in the circumstances, the Lord might pardon this lie. But before you go to see them, make sure they have been advised of Tommy's death by the War Office. You wouldn't want to be the one to unwittingly break the news to them.*

The battalion held the line at Villers-Bretonneux until August 1918 when the Allies launched a new offensive, the "Hundred Days Offensive", which ultimately brought about an end to the war. The 33rd was committed to the battle on 8th August and tasked with capturing Accroche Wood. A later series of advances followed, as the Allies broke through the German defences along the Hindenburg Line. After attacking around Road Wood in late August, the

33rd Battalion was withdrawn for three weeks rest before taking part in a joint American-Australian attack at Bellecourt in late September. Following up the Americans, the 33rd held off a strong counterattack by German forces around Gillemont Farm, before carrying out mopping-up operations towards Bony. Solomon and his stretcher-bearer partner found themselves retrieving wounded and killed Australian and American troops from the battlefield and, on occasions, wounded German soldiers. After this, in early October, the battalion was pulled back to the Abbeville area, taking up billets in Citerne, where they remained until the armistice was signed on 11th November 1918. During the course of the war, the 33rd Battalion had lost 451 men with 2,052 wounded. Two members of the battalion, Private John Carroll and Private George Cartwright, were amongst sixty-four Australians awarded the Victoria Cross during the First World War.

At war's end, on 11th November 1918, Solomon Schoupp was hospitalised, dangerously ill with exhaustion and pneumonia and, on 24th December 1918, he was repatriated from France to 1st Birmingham War Hospital, Rednal, England, where he spent the next three months recovering and recuperating. On 1st April 1919, he embarked from Southport, England, on the hospital ship *Strokshire* for repatriation to Australia. Ella and four-year-old Phyllis were there to greet him when he disembarked at Woolloomooloo's Finger Wharf in Sydney.

They stayed several nights in the Salvation Army's People's Palace in Sydney before commencing their train journey back to Glen Innes. During their stay in Sydney, Ella broke the news to Solomon that his grandmother, Sarah Woodbury, had passed away during the time he himself had been recuperating in the English War Hospital. Ella passed him an obituary cutting from a Tingha newspaper.

Obituary. Sarah Elizabeth Pate Woodbury.

There joined the silent majority Thursday night of last week, an old pioneer of the district, in Mrs Sarah Elizabeth Pate Woodbury, at the age of 81 years. The late Mrs Woodbury came from England at the early age of five years and resided with her parents about the Hawkesbury River. She was the relict of the late George James Woodbury who predeceased her some 14 years ago. The surviving children are: Matthew (Inverell), Mrs Love (Barraba), Mrs Aquilla Schoupp (Tingha), Mrs Norris, (Inverell). Mrs Long (Maitland), Solomon (Inverell), Abel (Tingha), and Amos (Inverell). Until quite recently the late Mrs Woodbury although so aged, had enjoyed good health. For more than a quarter of a century she had been a staunch member of the Salvation Army. The end came, not unexpectedly, Thursday afternoon at the home of her son, Mr Matthew Woodbury, Medora Street, Inverell. The funeral took place on Friday afternoon at 2 o'clock, when the Salvation Army Band led the cortege to the cemetery, where Adjutant Hawkins read the burial service.[2]

Solomon also learned, at that time that Ella's younger sister, Olive Ruth Nerney, had moved to Glen Innes in early 1919 to be close to Ella. There, Olive had met Hilton Andrew Currie Sweeney and the two were to be married in Glen Innes on 15th July 1919. Ella, Solomon and Phyllis would be back in Glen Innes just in time to attend the wedding. It would be the first occasion since Solomon and Ella's move to Glen Innes that they would come face to face with Ella's parents and it would be the first time Ernest and Mary Nerney had seen their granddaughter.

"Mother and Father will be staying with us for a few days while they're in Glen Innes for Ollie's wedding," Ella said. "Mother wrote and asked whether that would be all right."

"And you told them that'd be fine?"

"Yes. I hope I did the right thing. Do you mind?"

"Not at all," Solomon replied. "It could be a little tense, but it's something we need to face. They are, after all, your parents, and we need to do what we can to help put the relationship back on a normal footing."

"I'm glad you feel that way, Sol," his wife said. "I hope enough time has now passed to allow our family to move on."

Solomon nodded.

"And I hope we can also go and see my mother and the rest of my family in Tingha," he said. "It's time to put things right."

Ella squeezed Solomon's hand and rested her head on his shoulder.

"Things are going to work out, Sol. I know they are."

About two hours out of Sydney, the train left Gosford and turned inland, and Solomon found he could not help reflecting on the changing countryside, as views of the Hawkesbury and the central coast gave way to the drier vista of the broad-acre sheep and cattle grazing fields. As he watched it change, he thought about the changing phases of his own life. He saw his life as having been divided into two distinct phases by the Great War. The pre-war years had been bitter-sweet years — joyous times spent growing up with his family in Tingha, followed by his marriage to Ella and the gift of Phyllis, their first child. But that joy had also been fractured by the moral outrage which had resulted, understandably, because of Ella's pregnancy outside of marriage. He blamed himself for the estrangements that had occurred both within his own family and Ella's.

And now he was embarking on what he saw as the second phase of his life, the post-war phase. What did it hold for him, he wondered?

We have to move forward, he determined. *With the war behind us, we must re-establish a proper family basis — for our own sake, of course, but also for the sake of my mother in Tingha, for Ella's parents in Inverell, but most importantly for Phyllis and for the future children I hope we will have. I'll make a start on repairing those relationships when Ella's parents come to Glen Innes this week for Ollie's wedding.*

When the train stopped for ten minutes at Werris Creek station, Solomon hurried to the railway refreshment rooms where he purchased tea in plastic cups and a glass of milk for Phyllis. He hurried back to the train and had just enough time to rush back to the refreshment rooms again to buy sandwiches and fruit for their lunch.

As the train pulled out of the station, the three of them sat enjoying their lunch.

"Do you want to talk to me about the war, Sol?" Ella asked, when Phyllis seemed totally preoccupied, looking out the window at the passing countryside.

Solomon glanced at his little daughter, as tears welled up in his eyes. He shook his head.

"You don't want to know about it, Ell'," he said.

They sat in silence for a few more minutes before Solomon spoke again.

"It was madness, absolute madness, and I think I'll never be able to forget some of the things I saw. Governments are saying it was 'the war to end all wars'. We must pray it is so."

Later, as the train left Armidale and commenced the last leg of its journey to Glen Innes, Solomon began to think about the town he had left more than three years earlier when he had gone off to war and wondered how it had changed. Then when Ella mentioned the upcoming wedding again, it made him ponder why Olive had chosen to come to live in Glen Innes

"I must say I'm surprised that Ollie came to live in Glen Innes," he said to Ella. "Why did she do that?"

"My father sent her," Ella replied after a short pause. "I needed support."

Solomon thought about Ella caring for baby Phyllis while worrying about him every day, wondering whether he was safe, wondering every moment where he was, what he was doing and whether he was in danger. He knew about the psychological burden that war placed on wives and families on the home front and he could understand that Ella might have needed daily support to help her through such times. But when Ella had said "I needed support", she was speaking of something that went beyond the daily anguish of the unknown.

She reached for her handbag and took out a folded typed letter. She choked back her tears as she unfolded the letter and smoothed it against her handbag and then, with her voice faltering with emotion, she handed the letter to him.

"There were reports in the newspaper that you had died in hospital from pneumonia," she said. "I was beside myself with grief, and Ollie came to be with me. She was of enormous help to me at that time. But she also said to me, "This is not right, Ella. It is shameful that you have not been officially notified." So, the two of us sat down and wrote an angry letter to the War Office. Eventually, they sent me this letter."

9th January 1919

Dear Madam,
I have to acknowledge receipt of your letter dated 3rd instant, and to state no advice has been received here that your husband died of illness. The report which appeared in the press evidently referred to another member of the Australian Imperial Force. Since communicating with you on 30th ultimo advice has been received that your husband was transferred on 25/12/18 to 1st Birmingham War Hospital, Rednal, England, suffering from pneumonia. Any later cabled reports coming to hand will be promptly communicated to you at the address mentioned hereunder.

The letter was signed by the Officer-in-Charge of Base Records, Melbourne.

"You thought I was dead?" Solomon asked.

Ella nodded.

"Yes," she said. "That's why Father sent Ollie to Glen Innes."

Solomon was quiet for some time, sitting back and closing his eyes while the wheels of the train clacked rhythmically on the rails.

The man's something of a conundrum, he thought. *He's as tough as steel and was totally unyielding when we had to marry, yet he cared enough about Ella to send Olive to be with her at a time of need. It's going to be interesting to meet up with him again.*

1. The Tingha Advocate & North-Western Journal, Friday 21 Jul 1916, p. 2
2. The Tingha Advocate & North-Western Advocate, Friday 21 Feb 1919, p. 2.

Solomon James Schoupp & Margaret Ella Schoupp née Nerney

Ernest Thomas Nerney (1866–1948)

11
(1919 – 1939)

On 14th July 1919, Ella's parents, Ernest and Mary Nerney, arrived in Glen Innes to celebrate the marriage of their daughter, Olive Ruth Nerney, the next day. They were made welcome in the home of Solomon and Ella and would stay there until after the wedding. Both were besotted with little Phyllis, this being the first time they had ever seen her, and they were unrestrained in their love and affection for their daughter Ella. It had been a long and difficult period since they had last said goodbye to Solomon and Ella in Inverell, four and a half years earlier, and the joy of their reunion showed.

The day after the wedding, before he and his wife returned to Inverell, Ernest Nerney took Solomon aside for a chat on the veranda. Ella brought them tea and cake, but then withdrew, knowing the two men needed to spend some time together.

"We're so relieved to have you back safely from the war," Ernest said. "I can see you have a way to go with your physical recovery, and we can't even begin to imagine what effect the horrors of war may have had on your mind."

"Thank you, sir," Solomon replied in a quiet, noncommittal tone.

"Was it bad?" his father-in-law asked.

"War is folly, sir. It's an affront to everything civilised. But it's not something I really want to talk about."

"What *do* you want to talk about, Sol?"

"I want to thank you for sending Ollie to be with Ella during a very difficult time for her," he replied.

Ernest sipped his tea and nodded.

"We do love Ella, Solomon. We love her very much. You do realise that don't you?"

"I do, sir."

The two sat there in uncomfortable silence while Ernest struggled to find the right words.

"Four years ago," he eventually said, "we had to make a very difficult decision — one which I know was difficult and painful for my family and perhaps even more difficult and painful for you and Ella."

Solomon nodded.

"Ella and I were young," he said. "We made a mistake that had consequences beyond just the two of us. My own family in Tingha made the same decision, and I never saw my father again. As you know, my father died while I was in France. I understand my father's decision and I understand the decision you made. It was my fault, and I can only ask for your forgiveness."

Ernest was beginning to show signs of deep emotion. He had choked up and was unable to speak, and tears were welling up in his eyes. In a man such as he, it was quite extraordinary. When he spoke, he did so very quietly, in little more than a whisper.

"Who amongst us does not require forgiveness?" he asked.

It was the closest he could come to asking for forgiveness. The two men sat in silence, Solomon sipping his tea, while Ernest tried to regain his equilibrium.

"You know, Solomon," he finally said, still somewhat choked up, "war is not the only thing that could be called folly. Family pride is right up there too."

Solomon nodded but waited for his father-in-law to continue.

"We love Ella and we love you and Phyllis, Solomon. We'd love you to visit us in Inverell and stay for a while — for as long as you like."

It was an invitation expressed in hope, but without confidence that his son-in-law would accept. *Will he be prepared to make a fresh start — or will he seek retribution for the way I treated them at the time of their marriage,* he wondered.

"I'd like that, sir," Solomon replied. "I'd like that very much. But first we must visit my mother in Tingha."

"Of course!"

"We'll plan a visit there soon. Then, and after spending some time with my mother, perhaps we can go to

Inverell and stay with you and your family on our way back to Glen Innes."

Ernest reached out and took his son-in-law's hand.

"Thank you, son," he said.

Solomon had been medically discharged from the AIF on 1st July 1919. He received a small war service invalid pension, but he planned to return to work with the Glen Innes Municipal Council as soon as he could. The Glen Innes winter was exacerbating the nerve pains in his right leg and was making walking difficult for him because of the wound he had suffered on the Western Front. Doctors quite quickly realised that his right leg was somewhat shorter than his left, because of the less than satisfactory surgery he had undergone at the front-line hospital in France. From that time on, he always wore a shoe with a raised heel and a thicker sole on his right foot. He would wear those shoes and walk with a stick for the rest of his life.

He wrote to his mother, Aquilla, telling her that he, Ella and Phyllis would like to visit her in Tingha in the Spring, when the muddy roads would have dried out.

> *Ella and I long to see you after all these years. I hope that sufficient time has passed to ensure that we'll not bring any embarrassment to you because of our past mistake.*

A most gracious letter came in reply. Aquilla dearly wanted to see her son, her daughter-in-law and her granddaughter. She wrote back to them immediately.

> *It has been far too long. I cannot wait to see you all. Please come soon.*

Solomon, Ella and little Phyllis travelled by bus to Inverell at the beginning of September 1919 and made an immediate connection to a bus that would take them from Inverell to Tingha. When the bus pulled into the bus station in Tingha, they looked out the window and saw a large banner that read, "WELCOME HOME SOLOMON!" As they alighted from the bus, with Solomon carrying his young daughter, it seemed half of Tingha was there to meet them. In fact, it probably *was* half of Tingha — thirty people in all!

Apart from Solomon's mother, Aquilla, they were met by Solomon's sister, Sarah, with her husband John Cox and their five children; his sister, Emma, her husband Alfie Cox and their six children; his sister, Jessie, her husband Thomas Mildren and their seven children; his sister, Rhoda, her husband Alf Cooper and their two children; and Solomon's brother, George, who had never married.

Aquilla wrapped her arms around both Solomon and Ella and wept.

"At last!", she said through her tears. "At last, we're together again."

They stayed with Aquilla for three weeks, with Solomon taking every opportunity to catch up with friends, some of whom had worked with him in the mines. They attended the Sunday morning and evening Salvation Army services with Aquilla, and Solomon's brother, George. For Solomon, the enjoyment of catching up with family and friends was marred only by the absence of his father and, on the afternoon of their second Sunday in Tingha, he asked Aquilla to go with him to the cemetery to see his father's grave. Ella decided to give him that space, alone with his mother and father, and said she would go with him later.

Aquilla and Solomon took a small sprig of golden wattle and placed it below the simple headstone and, as they stood there, each with their own thoughts, Solomon asked his mother how his father's death had occurred.

"He truly didn't know it was coming," Aquilla said. "He was very well — here one day and gone the next. I suppose heart attacks are like that."

"I wish I'd been here," Solomon said. "It must have been very difficult for you."

"Well, the girls were here, and George" she told him. "They gathered around me and attended to everything that needed to be done. And Mr Nerney and his wife came immediately. It was nice to have them here at that time."

Solomon nodded.

"I'm glad they came," he said. "That was good of them, in the circumstances. They could have allowed their enmity towards me to have kept them away."

"Have you seen them, Sol?"

"Yes," he replied. "They were in Glen Innes about a month ago for Olive's wedding."

"And was it all right — between you and them, I mean?"

"Yes, it was all right. A little tense at times, but I had a good talk with Ella's father. I think it's going to be okay. In fact, we're planning to stay with them for a while in Inverell on our way home to Glen Innes."

"I'm glad, Sol," Aquilla said, squeezing his hand as they stood looking at his father's grave. "Family is too important to allow differences to divide us."

Solomon had to make one more visit before he left Tingha and he would make that visit alone. He knew he had to go and see old Tom McArdle and his wife, the parents of his friend, Tommy, who had been killed at Villers-Bretonneux. He chose to go on a Sunday afternoon when the grocery shop would be closed. When they opened the door to him, they knew who he was. They had heard he was in town and knew he would come. Nothing was said — nothing needed to be said. Instead, they simply embraced him tightly, and he them.

They led him into the house and sat down in comfortable armchairs. Mrs McArdle prepared tea and cake, but still nothing was said. All the three of them wanted was to sit there together, silently sharing their grief. Solomon was grateful Tommy's parents did not wish to know how their son had died, whether he had suffered and whether he had been a brave and courageous soldier. They had lost their only son — what did such questions matter? After an hour, Solomon rose to leave, and it was then that he said the only words he had spoken during the visit.

"I loved him like a brother."

They embraced him again and closed the door behind him.

Solomon, Ella and Phyllis left Tingha at the end of September, promising Aquilla and the others that they would visit whenever they could. They then moved on to the Nerney home in Inverell where they were made very welcome. Ernest and Mary Nerney doted on little Phyllis and took her to visit their friends in Inverell. They attended Salvation Army meetings with Ella's parents and enjoyed catching up with old friends who remembered them from their pre-marriage days. None, it seemed, thought anything of their hasty marriage and departure from Inverell. Many, especially the older men, wanted to talk to Solomon about his war experiences, but it was a topic he adroitly avoided as much as possible.

In mid-October, Solomon and Ella announced to Ella's parents that they needed to leave and return to Glen Innes.

"It's been a lovely visit," Solomon said, "and I thank you for being so welcoming towards us."

"Can't you stay longer?" Ernest asked.

"I'm sorry, sir. I need to return to Glen Innes and find some work. We can't live on my small war pension alone."

"Will it be hard to find work?"

"I doubt it. I'm well known in Glen Innes, and with my war service, I think I'll be well accepted."

"What about your leg and your difficulty walking?" Mary Nerney asked.

"Some work would be difficult for me because of that," her replied, nodding, "but I'm hoping I'll get work as a truck driver with the Municipal Council. I did that before the war, and I think I'll get my old job back."

"Well, if you need help in any way, just let us know," Ella's father said.

"Thank you, sir. We appreciate that."

"And," said Ella's mother then, pausing quite some time before deciding to go on, "we might have a surprise for you."

Solomon and Ella looked at her enquiringly.

"We're thinking that *maybe* we might move to Glen Innes," she told them.

Ella's mouth dropped open, and Solomon raised his eyebrows. It was indeed quite a surprise.

"Well, after all," Mary Nerney continued, "we have two daughters in Glen Innes now, and I'm sure there'll be lots more new grandchildren."

Solomon and Ella both broke into broad smiles.

"Oh, that'd be wonderful!" Ella exclaimed. "Ollie will be so happy too."

"How about you, Solomon?" Ernest asked. "How would you feel about that?"

After their successful visit and their acceptance by Ella's parents, Solomon had no issues about his in-laws moving closer. He knew Ernest would always be a stern father-in-law but, in a way, he respected that.

"I'd be delighted, sir," he replied. Then he added with a smile, "I'll save the big drum for you at the Salvation Army."

"Well, it's not going to happen this year," Ernest said, "Maybe next year. We'll see."

In Glen Innes, Solomon did indeed get his old job back, driving trucks for the Glen Innes Municipal Council, mostly delivering gravel and other materials for road maintenance sites. In all, Solomon would work for the Glen Innes Municipal Council for a total of thirty-four years. In 1920, Solomon and Ella purchased a home at 91 Church Street in Glen Innes and there they would raise their family and live out the rest of their lives.

A second daughter, Stella Iris Joan, who would always be known as Iris, was born on 8th December 1921. Twin boys followed on 13th March 1925 and were given the names Dudley Ernest George and Lionel Henry James.

The inclusion of the name "Ernest" in Dudley's name was a mark of respect to Ella's father. A third daughter, Mary Joyce, always to be known as Joyce, was born on 19th June 1931 and another daughter, Audrey June, arrived on 26th June 1933. The last of their children would be another daughter, Maureen Margaret, born on 16th March 1938.

Ernest and Mary Nerney made good on their promise to move to Glen Innes and, in January 1922, soon after the birth of Iris, they purchased a home in Meade Street. Sadly, Mary Nerney would not enjoy living close to her daughters or her grandchildren for very long. She died unexpectedly on 3rd August 1926 and was buried in the Salvation Army section of the Glen Innes cemetery. She was fifty-eight years of age.

Life was simple in Glen Innes and probably in most other rural towns during the inter-war years of the 1920s-1930s. In the early mornings, the milkman would come with his horse-drawn milk cart, to fill the jugs the homeowners had left on the doorstep. Small, beaded nets were always used on these jugs to keep the flies away. The milkman's horse didn't need to be driven — the milkman would merely click his tongue and the horse would amble along after him as he went from house to house. When the milkman and his horse had moved on, Solomon would go out and shovel up any horse manure, for his vegetable garden.

The butcher and the grocer both called for orders which they would deliver later in the day. The grocery boy from Mackenzie's department store would deliver the groceries on his bicycle in a large wicker basket attached to the front of the handlebars. The bread man also used a large basket to deliver bread that later had to be cut into thick slices, and the ice man came twice a week, using callipers to carry large blocks of ice for the icebox where perishable food had to be stored.

Households carefully recycled brown paper bags and string, and children sold newspaper to the butcher. Sticky rolls of flypaper hung from the ceiling, especially in the kitchen. And, in the evenings, the family would gather around the large cabinet radio and listen to *Blue Hills*, *The Children's Hour* and *The Argonauts Club*. Saturday mornings were often spent in Grey Street, the main street of Glen Innes — more a social event than a shopping trip. Very occasionally, if a film were deemed to be wholesome enough, the Schoupp children were allowed to attend Saturday afternoon matinees at either of the town's cinemas, the Grand Theatre in Grey Street or the Roxy in Meade Street.

The Schoupp family, together with Ernest Nerney, and his wife Mary, until her death in 1926, were always very active members of the Glen Innes Salvation Army. On Sunday evenings, all members of the Corps would gather in Grey Street for an open-air service, after which they would invite any interested listeners to join them at the Salvation Army Hall for a salvation service.

Phyllis, too, had become a very active soldier in the Glen Innes Corps of the Salvation Army. She taught Sunday School to young children and was often to be seen handing out copies of the Salvation Army newsletter, the *War Cry*, in the main street of Glen Innes. Yet, it still surprised her parents when, after a Sunday night service in 1936, she made a momentous announcement to them.

"God wants me to be in full time service with the Salvation Army," she said. "I want to go to the Salvation Army College and train to be an officer."

"Oh, Phyllis," her father said. "That's a huge step. I think you need to give this some more thought."

Her mother nodded in agreement.

"Dear, they could send you anywhere," Ella said. "We might never see you again, and I don't know how you'll live. Their officers are paid very little. And what about marriage? You're twenty years old now."

"I must answer God's call," Phyllis said. "He'll take care of everything else."

"Does God know you only went to school until the age of thirteen?" Solomon asked. "Will that be enough for the Army?"

"If God wants me, that will be enough," Phyllis replied. "God will equip me to do his work."

Phyllis entered the Salvation Army Training College in Petersham, Sydney, in 1937 and, after training, she would serve as a Salvation Army Officer for thirteen years, with appointments throughout New South Wales and Queensland. Her parents and her grandparents missed her greatly, but they were enormously proud of her.

Phyllis Jean Schoupp in the uniform of
a Salvation Army Officer.

On the night of Sunday, 3rd September 1939, the Schoupp family, like families across Australia, gathered around their large cabinet radio to listen to an announcement of national importance.

At the appointed time, there was a moment of silence, then the introduction by a radio announcer.

> *Ladies and gentlemen, the Prime Minister of Australia, Mr Robert Menzies.*

Listeners heard a faint rustle of papers as the Prime Minister sat down and settled at the microphone.

> *My fellow Australians*, he said, as people across the nation held their breath.

The Prime Minister's voice was clearly recognisable, thick and low, his English refined and his words statesmanlike but also ominous.

> *It is my melancholy duty to inform you officially that in consequence of a persistence by Germany in her invasion of Poland, Great Britain has declared war upon her and that, as a result, Australia is also at war.* [1]

Menzies spoke for another seventeen minutes, reminding Australians that Britain had done everything possible to avoid this war and declaring that the German Führer had embarked on a war of his own making and had done so on the back of broken promises and dishonoured agreements. Menzies made it clear to his listeners that Australia stood side by side with the United Kingdom. He did not add that it did so, not as a matter of choice, but as a consequence of the Australian Constitution under which, by law, The Commonwealth of Australia was compelled to support the United Kingdom in any act of war. Such had been the case at the outbreak of the First World War, and so it was again, twenty-five years later.

There can be no doubt that where Great Britain stands, there stands the people of the entire British world," Menzies continued. *"Bitter as we all feel at this wanton crime, this is not a moment for rhetoric … I know that in spite of the emotions we are all feeling, you will show that Australia is ready to see it through. May God in his mercy and compassion grant that the world may soon be delivered from this agony.*[2]

Australia was at war with Germany — again.

A little over a year after Australia went to war against Germany, Solomon's mother, Aquilla Schoupp, passed away in Tingha. It was 6th December 1940, and the entire Schoupp family from Glen Innes travelled to Tingha for the funeral service at the Tingha Salvation Army. Aquilla was buried next to her husband in the Tingha cemetery.

1. Australian War Memorial collection https://www.awm.gov.au/articles/encyclopedia/prime_ministers/menzies (accessed June 2022).
2. Ibid

12
(1939 – 1943)

Listening to that same broadcast on 3rd September 1939, some two hundred miles north of Glen Innes, as they gathered around their tiny mantle radio was the small family of a Bundamba Blacksmith — Percy White, his wife Mary Jane and their two daughters, Ruby May and Florence.

Although they had absolutely no connection to the Schoupp family in Glen Innes, the White family were also adherents of the Salvation Army and regularly attended meetings at the Bundamba Corps. It was really the eldest child, Ruby, who was the most fervent soldier of the Salvation Army in the White family, and the rest of them had been drawn into becoming uniform wearing soldiers under her influence. Both Ruby and Florence played timbrels in Salvation Army open-air meetings and in meetings within the hall, and Percy played a cornet in the band. Percy was a gifted man in several ways, including musically. He was self-taught on the cornet and when his wife asked him why he was joining the band, he replied, "Well, it's something I can do, and those Salvos at Bundamba need all the musical help they can get." Soon thereafter, Percy became the Corps' bandmaster.

At the end of Prime Minister Menzies's seventeen-minute address to the nation, Percy turned off the radio and the family sat in silence for a few moments, trying to take in the enormity of what they had heard. It was Florence who eventually broke the silence.

"What does it mean for us, Dad?" she asked her father.

"I don't think it means anything for us, Flo'. I'm too old to go to war. I just hope your brother's not stupid enough to enlist. Far too many good Australian men died fighting the last war in Europe — a war that really shouldn't have concerned us."

"It doesn't seem to make much sense for Australian men to go off and fight on the other side of the world," Florence said.

"It doesn't need to make sense, Flo," Percy replied. "It's politics."

The one person missing from the White family as they listened to the Prime Minister's broadcast that night was Percy and Mary's second child and only son, James Edward, always known as Jim. It was Jim that Percy had been referring to when he expressed the hope that Ruby and Florence's brother would not be stupid enough to enlist.

Jim White had been born in Ipswich on 28th January 1918 and he, too, had joined his father in playing a cornet in the Salvation Army band. Growing up in his father's blacksmith workshop behind their small house at the back of the Bundamba racecourse, he picked up many of the creative traits of his father. There was not much either of them could not make. Jim had received little schooling although he was certainly literate and, surprisingly, he was quite good with simple mathematical calculations.

At fifteen years of age, Jim left home and moved to Mackay in North Queensland to take work planting and cutting sugar cane.

Fig.1 Jim White, second from left, planting sugar cane at Yalboroo, near Mackay, North Queensland, c. 1937

Jim was probably one of the few Australians who did not hear the Prime Minister's speech on the radio that Sunday night, 3rd September 1939. In the sheds the owner of the canefields provided for their accommodation, the workers had no radio. It was a week later, on Sunday 10th September, that Jim and his workmates went into Mackay, planning to have a counter-lunch at a hotel. And there they saw a newspaper with a bold headline — **AUSTRALIA AT WAR!**

With his two workmates, Jim read the report about German forces invading Poland and about Britain's declaration of war against Germany.

"Why does that mean Australia is at war?" one of his mates asked.

None of them knew the answer to that question and the three immediately decided that a European war was none of their concern. In Bundamba, Percy would have been pleased. But war was coming, and it would soon engulf Australia.

In March 1940, Jim made a weekend trip back to Bundamba for the wedding of his younger sister, Florence. Flo had met a young man at the Bundamba Salvation Army and the two were married on 21st March 1940. Jim's new brother-in-law was Wallace Dudley James McLaren, known simply as Wal. He worked at Krugers Sawmill in Ipswich and, though it was a short meeting, he and Jim hit it off immediately. Jim and Wal would remain close for the rest of their lives.

Shortly after Prime Minister Menzies' historic announcement that Australia was at war with Germany, the Australian Labor Party, led by John Curtin, had declined to enter a war cabinet led by Prime Minister Menzies. Curtin did, however, offer bipartisan co-operation, provided it did not extend to conscription for overseas service. Curtin and the Labor Party narrowly lost the September 1940 election, and the Menzies-led UAP-Coalition was sworn in as a minority government relying upon the support of two independents.

In January 1941, Menzies flew to Britain to discuss the weakness of Singapore's defences with Winston Churchill's British War Cabinet. Returning to Australia, with the threat of a belligerent Japan in the air and with the Australian army having suffered badly in the Greek and Crete campaigns, Menzies re-approached the Labor Party to form a War Cabinet. Curtin again declined and, in mid-September, the two independents announced that the Menzies government could no longer count on their support in the House of Representatives. The Governor-General, Lord Gowrie, was reluctant to call another election during a time of war and, when the independents agreed to support the Curtin-led Labor Party, John Curtin was sworn in as Prime Minister of Australia on 7th October 1941. Two months later, on 7th December 1941, the forces of the Empire of Japan attacked the American fleet at anchor in Pearl Harbor, in the Hawaiian Islands.

Sunday 7th December 1941, a date that the American President Franklin Delano Roosevelt declared would "live in infamy" is often remembered as the attack on the American fleet at Pearl Harbor. It is less often remembered as the commencement of the Japanese attacks through the whole western Pacific.

Admiral Isoroku Yamamoto's plan called for two simultaneous operations. The first operation, to which he committed all six of his regular aircraft carriers, two battleships, three cruisers and eleven destroyers, was to be a surprise attack, scheduled for 7th December (8th December by Western Pacific time), on the main US Pacific Fleet in its base at Pearl Harbor. The rest of the Japanese Navy was to support the Japanese army in what Yamamoto called the "Southern Operation". Eleven infantry divisions and seven tank regiments, supported by 795 combat planes, launched two drives, one from Formosa (Taiwan) through the Philippines, the other from French Indochina (Vietnam) and Hainan Island through the Malaya peninsula and Singapore to occupy the islands of the Dutch East Indies (Indonesia), particularly Sumatra, Java and Borneo, with their rich resources of oil, tin and rubber. During the drive south, Wake Island, Guam, the Gilbert Islands, Burma and Thailand were all secured in what was an audacious and largely successful offensive.

The speed of the Japanese occupations through south-east Asia and the western Pacific was nothing less than astonishing. If the world had thought the German *blitzkrieg* through western Europe had been fast, the Japanese racked it up a notch, and more. On the very day of the Pearl Harbor attack, 8th December 1941 by Western Pacific time, Japanese bombers from Formosa struck Clark and Iba airfields in the Philippines, destroying more than fifty percent of the US Army's Far East aircraft. Two days later, another attack destroyed yet more US fighters and the Cavite Naval docks. The Philippines would eventually surrender to the Japanese on 8th May 1942.

Again, on the day of the Pearl Harbor attack, 8th December 1941, the Japanese 25th Army of the Imperial Japanese Army moved out of Indochina and launched amphibious assaults on the Malay Peninsula, landing in the north at Khota Bharu in Malaya and at Pattani and Songkhla in Thailand. Thailand fought against the Japanese for only five hours before calling for a ceasefire and then forming an alliance with Japan, making Thailand part of the Axis powers until the end of World War II.

The Gilbert Islands were surrendered to the Japanese on 9th December 1941, the Solomon Islands on the same day, Guam on 10th December 1941, and Wake Island on 23rd December 1941.

On 26th December 1941 John Curtin made a speech that was broadcast to the nation on radio and reprinted in all major newspapers the next day.

> *Without any inhibitions of any kind, I make it quite clear that Australia looks to America, free of any pangs*

as to our traditional links or kinship with the United Kingdom. We know the problems that the United Kingdom faces ... But we know, too, that Australia can go, and Britain can still hold on. We are, therefore, determined that Australia shall not go, and shall exert all our energies towards the shaping of a plan, with the United States as its keystone, which will give to our country some confidence of being able to hold out until the tide of battle swings against Japan.[1]

Curtin clearly saw the entry of the United States into the Pacific war as Australia's saviour. In this speech, he turned Australia's strategic policy for the defence of Australia away from reliance on the United Kingdom and thereafter focused on building a strategic alliance with the United States. Churchill was infuriated.

After their invasion of the Malay peninsula at Khota Bharu on 8th December, the Japanese 25th Army under the command of General Tomoyuki Yamashita immediately turned south. Kuala Lumpur was taken on 11th January and Johore Bahru, capital of Malaya's southern state, fell on 14th January. The Japanese had fought the seven hundred miles from their northern landings, through what the British defence planners had believed to be totally impenetrable jungle, to the southern tip of the peninsula in just six weeks.

After retreating across the causeway linking Jahore Bharu and the so-called island fortress of Singapore and blowing up the causeway behind them, the British, Australian and Indian forces in Singapore prepared to defend the island.

The battle for Singapore lasted just eight days before the British commander, Lieutenant General Arthur Percival, surrendered Singapore on 15th February 1942. More than 130,000 Allied troops were taken prisoner. Of those, more than 15,000 were Australians, approximately 7,000 of whom would die as prisoners of war, forced to work on building the Japanese army's infamous Thai-Burma railway.

Simultaneously, The Japanese invasion of the Dutch East Indies (Indonesia) began on 10th January 1942, and the Imperial Japanese Army overran the entire archipelago in less than three months. By mid-January 1942, parts of Sulawesi and Borneo were under Japanese control. By February, the Japanese had landed on Sumatra and occupied the rich oil-fields and the Royal Dutch Shell oil refineries at Palembang in South Sumatra. On 28th February and 1st March 1942, Japanese troops landed at four places along the northern coast of Java, virtually unopposed, and the pathway to New Guinea and Australia lay wide open.

In Bundamba, Percy White read news of the fall of Singapore from *The Worker*.

> *The fall of Singapore and the surrender of the fortress to its encircling foes is, without doubt, the heaviest blow that has yet been inflicted on Australia since the present war began, leaving as it does our shores practically wide open to the enemy, and involving the loss of approximately 13,000 of our own soldiers, who were involved in the surrender. These dire consequences, bad enough as they are, are not all of the evils that have overtaken our unhappy country. There is in addition the deep and very disturbing feeling that permeates the whole community,*

> *that we have been badly "let down," and Australia has been sadly betrayed by an unbelievable incompetence in Empire administration which has been worse than tragic.*[2]

In Glen Innes, Solomon Schoupp read from the *Glen Innes Examiner*.

> *According to official Tokio* [sic] *radio tonight, the first move was made by three officers bearing a white flag to the Japanese lines. Their proposals were rejected after which for two hours the Japanese continued their attack. Then General Percival, accompanied by Major C.H. Wilde and other members of his staff, motored to the Ford plant, where they met General Yamashita and others. General Yamashita told General Percival; "I wish your replies to be brief and to the point. I will listen only to an offer of unconditional surrender."*
> *General Percival: "Will you give me until tomorrow?"*
> *General Yamashita: "I cannot wait."*
> *General Percival: "Give me five hours."*
> *General Yamashita: "Then we will continue the attack meanwhile."*
> *General Percival remained silent. General Yamashita insisted on an answer, and General Percival finally and softly said "Yes".* [3]

In Mackay, North Queensland, Jim White read from the *Daily Mercury*.

> *It would be useless to deny that the news, yesterday of the fall of Singapore brought aching hearts to many and*

anxious minds to all. So many of the gallant defenders of the city are our own kith and kin that we have a local affinity with the tragic, historic episode, as well as a national relationship to the consequences of the surrender. The courage with which our men held the flag aloft until the interests of the civil population, who were being caught in the holocaust, caused them to succumb will be forever a vivid narrative when the feats of brave men are recalled to inspire humanity... ...Singapore can do for us what Dunkirk did for the English, and if the same stiffening of our resolve is the price of our retreat at this point, then in the long run Singapore will be looked upon in history as the current equivalent of Gallipoli.[4]

"This puts our country at risk," Jim told his mates. "I reckon the Japs have got their eyes on Australia now. I'm going home to Bundamba, to sign up."

Five days later, Jim White was back in Bundamba and, after brief discussions with his father, he enlisted in the 2nd AIF and became part of the 61st Battalion.

Whilst the Japanese 25th Army had been fighting its way down the Malay peninsula towards Singapore, two divisions of combat-hardened Australian troops were on the high seas, having been withdrawn from the Middle East with the intent of providing reinforcements for the defence of Singapore. Before they arrived, however, Singapore had already fallen and the British Prime Minister, Winston Churchill, had then ordered the ship to divert to Burma to reinforce Burma against the expected, and imminent, Japanese attack. Churchill was determined to defend Burma and so protect India, the jewel in British colonial possessions, from Japanese occupation. The Australian Prime Minister, John Curtin, however, demanded that Churchill's order be countermanded and insisted that the Australian troops be brought home for the defence of Australia. Churchill was even further incensed but Curtin insisted — "Australian troops will defend Australia."

"Missus White! Missus White!"

The voice came from the road in front of the White family's simple house in Station Road, Bundamba.

"Missus White! Missus White!"

Exiting from the front door of the house, Mary White saw her neighbour from a few doors up the road, Marcie Henderson, calling for her attention.

"What is it, Marcie?" she asked.

"It's y' boy! It's Jimmy! I just saw 'im at the cinema. The Movietone News has a segment 'bout the fightin' in New Guinea, and Jimmy was there. I'd know 'im anywhere."

"Was he all right? He wasn't injured, was he?"

"No," Marcie replied. "'e looked good. A bit tired maybe, 'nd a bit muddy, but 'e's okay."

Mary White thanked Marcie and hurried off to the cinema, determined to make the next session. The *Movietone News* began, as usual, before the main feature and a film of Australian soldiers on the Kokoda Track soon came on the screen. Mary watched closely and listened to the narrator's words.

> *There's a dramatic reality about all this that cannot be escaped,* the narrator read, *cheerfulness and courage, contrasting sharply with suffering. It will take a lot of Japs to conquer that kind of spirit.* [5]

As Mary watched, sure enough, there was her son Jim trying to walk up the Kokoda Track, his army boots sinking up to the ankles in mud. He was wearing khaki shorts, a short sleeved shirt and a steel helmet and carrying his rifle. He appeared in the film clip for all of three seconds but, after seeing that clip, Mary had no interest in staying for the feature film. She rushed home to tell Percy and, the next morning, the two of them went to the cinema together to see the *Movietone News* again. Mary White went to the cinema every day until that edition of *Movietone News* was replaced with a different film clip.

In August 1942, as part of the 61st Infantry Battalion, Jim had arrived in Milne Bay at the south-east tip of New Guinea, just in time to assist in repelling the Japanese amphibious landing on 27th August. After the battle for Milne Bay, part of the 7th Brigade, which included the 61st Infantry, moved to Port Moresby to defend that crucial city port against Japanese attack.

Having had their amphibious attack on Port Moresby thwarted by the US Navy in the battle of the Coral Sea, the Japanese then turned their efforts to an overland attack on Port Moresby from the rear. Japanese forces landed at Gona and Buna on the north coast of the New Guinea peninsula with the objective of seizing Port Moresby by following the Kokoda Track over the mountains of the Owen Stanley Range. And why not? The Japanese army, in advancing down the Malay peninsula to take Singapore, had shown their ability to push through what was thought to be impenetrable jungle, and there was no reason to doubt they could do a similar thing in the Owen Stanley Range. From Port Moresby, the Japanese army and air force would have been directly able to threaten Australia. The 39th Battalion and part of the 61st Battalion, 2nd AIF, were sent up the Kokoda track from Port Moresby, tasked with first halting the Japanese advance, then driving them back. The Japanese continually pushed the Australian troops back and advanced to within sight of Port Moresby but, by the end of September, they had outrun their supply line and the tide began to turn. The Australians pursued the Japanese back up the Kokoda Track, encountering strong opposition, but major battles around Oivi and Gorari from 4th to 11th November saw a decisive victory for the Australians. The Japanese offensive against Port Moresby had been defeated.

In the *Movietone News* clip of the 61st on the Kokoda Track, Jim White may have "looked good" to Marcie Henderson, but he wasn't. That footage had been shot in late-October 1942 and, by that time, the 61st had been on the Kokoda Track for almost three months. Jim, like many of his comrades, was suffering seriously from malaria. He was evacuated to Port Moresby from the small village of Kokoda in late October, before the battles of Oivi and Gorari, and was subsequently repatriated to Australia.

The Australian Army Medical Corps believed that men recovering from malaria would benefit from a cool climate and, in their wisdom, they chose Glen Innes where a large Army staging post had been established at the Glen Innes Golf Course, about five miles from town.

1. Hopkins W. B. *THE PACIFIC WAR — The Strategy, Politics, and Players That Won the War*, Zenith Press, imprint of MBI Publishing Company, Minneapolis, 2008, p.96. First published in The Herald, Melbourne, 27 December 1942.
2. *The Worker*, Brisbane, Qld, 17 February 1942, p.4
3. *Glen Innes Examiner,* 17 February 1942, p.1
4. *Daily Mercury*, Mackay, Qld, 17 February 1942, p.4
5. https://aso.gov.au/titles/newsreels/kokoda-front-line/clip1/

13
(1943 – 1947)

The walk into town from the Glen Innes golf links took about an hour and a half. It was a relatively flat road and, compared to the Kokoda Track, it was little more than a pleasant stroll. Furthermore, if he were lucky, once Jim reached the corner of Golf Links Road and the New England Highway, about halfway to town, he might pick up a lift from a passing farmer heading into town. Jim walked into town twice a week. Mid-week, he would walk into town for no other reason than to get the exercise and build up his strength as he recovered. The Medical Officer encouraged this exercise and Jim was given leave each Wednesday to do it, but with a warning — "Don't overdo it. Unnecessary exertion can cause a recurrence of malaria." Often, on those Wednesday visits to town Jim would have lunch at the Paragon Café in Grey Street.

On Sundays, or at least most Sundays, he and some other soldiers would walk into town to attend church services. Services conducted by the Army chaplains were held on base, but the young men yearned for civilian company, perhaps especially young female company. Jim and a couple of his friends from the Army encampment attended services at the Glen Innes Salvation Army. Quite apart from the fact that Jim had been raised Salvation Army, the young soldiers had seen and appreciated the work done by the Salvation Army in support of the troops in New Guinea. Because of that, some who had no prior association with the Salvation Army became regular attendees at the meetings in Glen Innes. Whether they were there to hear the word of God or to seek female company, is another issue.

It was, of course, at the Glen Innes Salvation Army that Jim met the Schoupp family. Solomon and Ella, together with their children, Iris, aged 21, and the twin boys, Dudley and Lionel, aged 17, were all active and zealous soldiers of the Glen Innes Salvation Army. The younger children, Joyce, Audrey and Maureen were still only school age — Joyce was twelve, Audrey ten, and Maureen just five.

At Salvation Army meetings in Glen Innes, Solomon, a large man in uniform, made a practice of approaching all visiting young men from the golf links camp and making them feel welcome.

"Solomon Schoupp," he'd say, reaching out his big hand. "Welcome boys! Glad to have you with us."

There would always be some friendly chat about life at the golf links camp, and Solomon would always follow it up with an invitation to his home.

"We always have 'open home' on Sundays for any of you boys. Our meals are simple, but the fellowship is warm. We'd be delighted if you would join us for lunch."

So it was that Jim and several of his mates found themselves regular visitors to the Schoupp family house on Sunday afternoons. Many of the soldiers who came to the Schoupp family's 'open house' had little, if any, association with the Salvation Army, yet all were made welcome. Jim White, however, now a young man of 24 years, had been a soldier of the Salvation Army since the days of his youth and, because of that, he felt a closer affinity with the family, and they with him. He was almost like an adopted son to them. But there was something that drew Jim and the Schoupp family closer together — a blossoming romance between Jim White and Iris Schoupp.

Stella Iris Joan Schoupp, always known as Iris, was still living at home with her parents in 1942. She had received minimal education up to the age of fifteen and had then worked as housekeeper for a Mrs Wharton who lived only a few doors further up the street from their home. Two days a week, she cleaned house for Mrs Wharton, did the laundry and carried the heavy rugs outside where she would hang them over the clothesline and beat them to remove any dust. Mrs Wharton was a kindly lady and Iris became quite fond of her. Indeed, after Mrs Wharton's death, Iris continued working for her son, Eric Wharton and his wife, and she would continue a long association with the Wharton family even after her marriage.

Living next-door to the Schoupp family at number 93 Church Street were Mr and Mrs Hunt who owned a café in Grey Street known simply as Hunt's Café. It was a popular café that offered probably the nicest cakes and the best meals in town, so when Mrs Hunt offered Iris the opportunity to work in the shop three days a week, Iris was delighted. Together with her work for Mrs Wharton, it would mean she would be working five days a week.

Another who was delighted with this development was Jim White. He immediately stopped having his Wednesday lunches at the Paragon Café and switched his patronage to Hunt's Café.

"You must realise you can't just stand there and talk to me all day at the café," Iris told him. "If you do that, you'll get me sacked."

"No, I won't do that," he replied. "I'll just sit there and eat my meal and watch you. I can't take my eyes off you."

"And when you've finished your meal?"

Jim shrugged and winked at her.

"Then I'll order another meal," he said with his cheeky smile that always made her giggle.

Christmas Day 1942 saw a large gathering at the home of the Schoupp family in Church Street. Of course, Solomon, Ella, and six of their seven children were present, the exception being Phyllis who, at that time, was serving as a Salvation Army officer in Moree. Ella's father, Ernest Nerney was also present, together with the large family of Ella's sister, Olive Sweeney. Olive and Hilton Sweeney had built their home in West Avenue on the other side of town and lived there with their twelve children. To that large family group were added Jim White and several of his mates from the golf links Army camp. It was a wonderful and joyous day.

Jim White and a few of his mates from the golf links camp had, over time, become an almost integral part of the Schoupp family and were sometimes included in family discussions. One such discussion occurred in early January 1943 during an "open house" lunch at which Ella's father was also present. One of the family's twin boys, Dudley, had decided that he felt called to follow his sister, Phyllis, into full time service as a Salvation Army officer. Solomon and Ella were not totally convinced it was a good idea, and it was a matter that generated a lot of discussion around the meal table.

"We've already got one of our children serving God as a Salvation Army officer," Ella said. "It makes it so hard for us to see her. I don't remember the last time I saw my daughter and I miss her so much. You can understand that, can't you, Jim?"

"I do understand, Mrs Schoupp. I've been a Salvationist most of my life. I've seen the work the officers do and how they get moved from place to place. They do wonderful work, but it's not easy and they're paid a pittance for it."

Solomon nodded.

"They certainly don't do it for the money," he said. "But, if Dudley believes he needs to serve God in this way, then I suppose we can't really stand in his way. Yet, he's so young, only seventeen, and I think we'd really prefer him to wait a few years."

"I want to give God the best years of my life," Dudley said, "and that's now, while I'm young."

"Well," said Steve, one of Jim's army mates, "I'm not Salvation Army myself, but I saw the Salvos in Port Moresby supporting the troops with soup kitchens, cups of tea, biscuits and even blankets. They were always there to share a friendly chat with us and they even had some signs of encouragement erected at places along the Track. God knows how they got the signs up there though. I have enormous respect for them, so I say, if that's what you believe you're called to do, Dudley, go for it!"

Ernest Nerney said nothing but glared across the table at Steve with a stern look of disapproval. Jim picked up on that look and elbowed Steve in the ribs, trying to show him he might have spoken out of turn and said too much about what was essentially a family matter.

But Dudley did answer his call and, in January 1943, at the age of just seventeen, he boarded the train from Glen Innes to Sydney and entered the Salvation Army Training College in Livingstone Road, Petersham, with the full blessing of his parents.

As for Jim and Iris, their romantic relationship continued to blossom, and they were beginning to talk of marriage when, in February 1943, the army suddenly intervened and transferred Jim back to the Chermside army base in Brisbane. He did everything possible to avoid being transferred back to Chermside, even appealing to the Medical Officer and claiming he was still suffering the effects of malaria, but the MO was unmoved.

"Sorry, son," the MO told him, "I can't swing it for you any longer. You're fit for service."

"I'll miss you," Iris said to him at the Glen Innes railway station, as he boarded the train back to Brisbane. "I'll write to you."

"I'll write too," Jim promised, "and I'll be back. I'm going to marry you."

He shook Solomon's hand, embraced Ella, then kissed Iris, before climbing aboard. As the train pulled out of the station, he leaned out the window, waving.

"I'll be back soon," he called to Iris. "I promise! The Army can't keep us apart for long."

Fig. 1 Stella Iris Joan Schoupp (known as Iris)

Fig. 2. Private James Edward White, 61st Battalion 2AIF

Jim soon discovered, however, that the Army could indeed keep them apart. In fact, the Army could do pretty much whatever it wanted to do. Life at the Chermside barracks was much more rigidly regulated than had been the case at the Glen Innes golf links camp and Jim was given weekend leave passes only twice a month. He and Iris wrote letters to each other several times a week, but it was not enough for either of them. With no telephone at the Schoupp family home in Glen Innes, corresponding by letters was their only option. Jim had not seen his parents or his sisters since his enlistment in February 1942 and he used his first weekend pass to visit them in Bundamba. With his second weekend pass, he travelled to Glen Innes to see Iris, but the travelling time to and from Glen Innes meant precious little time together.

"It's so hard, being able to be together like this for only such a short time," Iris told Jim tearfully, as they headed to the train platform once more, to say goodbye.

"It's even worse when I have to spend so many hours getting here and back," Jim grumbled. "Not that it isn't worth it when I see you, Iris, but… well, you know what I mean."

"I understand you need to see your own family as often as you can, Jim," Iris said then, her voice shaking, "but… well, do you think you can come down here again next time you get weekend leave?"

He hardly knew what to say at that point — he almost felt like crying himself. His heart sank at another long trip south, but he wanted to see Iris so much — he needed to. Yet he remembered too the look in his parents' eyes when he had visited them. That had almost made him cry too — they were not getting any younger and missed him so much.

He took a deep breath then and reached out to Iris, holding her close.

"Of course, I'd love to see you again as soon as possible, Iris, but… well, I know my parents want to see me too. Still, I'll try and write to them as soon as I can and explain how we feel. I do wish we lived nearer each other though — it's all so frustrating."

In April 1943, Jim's frustration got the better of him and he took off from Chermside, AWOL — Absent Without Official Leave — to go and visit Iris in Glen Innes. He stayed there for ten days before Solomon Schoupp persuaded him to return to the Army barracks in Chermside.

"You're going to be in trouble when the miliary catches up with you, Jim," he said, "and they will catch up with you."

"Probably," Jim replied flippantly, "but I'll make the most of my time until then."

Solomon, however, was quite serious.

"Jim, being absent without official leave is a serious offence with harsh punishments, especially during war time. It'll be better for you if you return and give yourself up to the authorities, rather than wait for them to come for you."

Jim took some convincing before he reluctantly returned to Chermside, where he found the military police waiting for him. He faced a court martial on 7th May 1943 and was lucky to receive a relatively minor punishment — twenty-eight days in the stockade, with hard labour.

"You were lucky!" his commanding officer said to him on his return to Chermside. "You'll not get off so lightly if you go AWOL again."

Soon after his release from the stockade, Jim was surprised to suffer his first relapse of malaria. The Medical Officer told him that malaria infects the liver and that those attacks can recur repeatedly for many years. It can particularly recur after periods of exertion and it most likely had been triggered, the MO told him, by the hard labour he had endured in the stockade. In November 1943, he suffered a second recurrence of malaria and, after recovering and recuperating, was medically discharged from the Army on 10th February 1944. He immediately announced to his family that he intended to return to Glen Innes and live with the Schoupp family, but his mother was less than pleased.

"We've seen so little of you since the war began," she protested. "Even since you've been back in Chermside, we've rarely seen you because you take off whenever possible to go and see that girl in Glen Innes. I don't know what's got into you!"

"Her name is Iris," Jim reminded her, "and she's not just 'that girl'. She's become very important to me."

"Your place is here with your family," his mother argued, "not chasing off after some girl you met during the war."

But Jim was in love.

"I'm sorry you feel that way, Mum," he said, "but I must return to Iris, and to Glen Innes. This is my home and I love you and all our family, but Iris is my future."

Jim left Bundamba and returned to Glen Innes, fully aware that his mother resented his decision. It was, perhaps a portent of difficult times ahead.

In Glen Innes, Jim and Solomon would often sit drinking tea on the front veranda of the Church Street home, watching the passing traffic. Church Street was, in fact, part of the New England Highway, the inland route linking Sydney and Brisbane.

"What's the significance of that copper sign?" he asked Solomon one day, pointing to a beaten copper plate near the front door bearing the word "*Marathon*".

"Marathon?" Solomon replied. "It was the name of the ship that took me to Europe for the First World War. Ella had it made when I returned."

Jim nodded, thinking about the fact that this ship had obviously been important enough to Ella to name their house after it.

I guess different things are important to different people, he thought. *I can't even remember the name of the ship that took me to Milne Bay. Not even sure I ever knew.*

"Seems to me it would've made more sense if she'd ordered a sign with the name 'Strokshire'," Solomon continued. "That was the ship that brought me home to Australia. But there you go — I guess women sometimes see things differently."

The two men sat dipping their hard Anzac biscuits in their tea for some time before Jim changed the subject.

"Iris and I would like to get married, sir," he said. "I'd like to ask your blessing for that."

Solomon was not surprised. He had known this was coming and had already discussed it with Ella.

"And when would you like this to happen?" he asked.

"As soon as possible, sir. As you know, we've known each other for a year and a half now and we're both committed to each other."

Solomon nodded and sipped his tea contemplatively before answering.

"Don't you think you should find a job before you marry, Jim? You'll need an income to support a wife and any children that come along."

"I've got that planned, sir. I have a brother-in-law, Wal McLaren, in Bundamba who works at Krugers Sawmill. Wal says that Krugers are very good at providing work for returned soldiers. They consider it part of their war effort and Wal assures me I'd get a job at Krugers. It seems like a good opportunity."

Solomon remained silent for some minutes before replying. He thought about his own marriage, precipitated by Ella's pregnancy out of wedlock, and he realised that delaying his approval could, possibly, result in Iris and Jim finding themselves in that same unhappy predicament

"I suppose we hadn't anticipated you'd be taking Iris away from Glen Innes, although we should have realised that would be a possibility," Solomon said. "As you know, both Phyllis and Dudley have left home to serve as Salvation Army officers. Ella misses them greatly and she'll certainly miss Iris. I will too, of course — but yes, you have our blessing."

James Edward White and Stella Iris Joan Schoupp were married at the Glen Innes Salvation Army on 8th April 1944 and a small reception was held at the home of the Schoupp family in Church Street. The day after the wedding, amidst tearful farewells at the Glen Innes railway station, Iris and Jim boarded the train that would take them to Roma Street Station in Brisbane. From there they would make the short journey back to Bundamba.

It was the first time Iris had met Percy and Mary White and Jim's sister Ruby who was still living at home. She found the house in Station Road, Bundamba, to be small, old and somewhat dilapidated compared to her family home in Glen Innes and permeated by the smell of Percy's pipe tobacco. Percy was rarely seen without his pipe, and the smell drifted along wherever he went. He used his pocketknife to shave his tobacco from a hard slab of tobacco, something akin to a cake of soap. In the process, of course, shavings of tobacco fell to the floor and the table and were left there until Ruby cleaned them up later. Iris also had the uneasy sense that Mary White resented her daughter-in-law's presence in the family home.

Wal McLaren was as good as his word and promptly spoke to the management at Krugers Sawmill about taking on his brother-in-law, Jim. Within a week of arriving back in Bundamba, Jim was working alongside Wal at Krugers Sawmill.

Iris, for her part, found a kindred spirit in Flo McLaren, Wal's wife and Jim's younger sister. They liked each other immediately and took every opportunity to spend time together. The two would remain close friends for the rest of their lives.

Fig. 2. The White family home in Station Road, Bundamba, with Percy White in the front yard.

Fig, 3, Jim (left) and Wal McLaren (right) working a crosscut chain saw at Krugers sawmill.

Tuesday 8th May 1945 was VE Day, marking the surrender of the forces of NAZI Germany and the end of the war in Europe. The streets of Britain, and particularly London, erupted in a spontaneous outbreak of celebrations that continued well into the night, with parties, singing and dancing. Winston Churchill declared the day a public holiday and many bonfires and fireworks were lit to mark the occasion

In Australia, the news was widely welcomed but celebrations were subdued because the war in the Pacific against the Empire of Japan was ongoing. Australians and the men and women of other allied nations were still dying in the struggle against the Japanese forces, and large-scale celebrations in those circumstances were considered inappropriate.

Prime Minister John Curtin who had led Australia throughout most of the Second World War passed away at The Lodge in Canberra on the evening of 5th July 1945. He was succeeded by Mr Ben Chifley who took over the office of Prime Minister on 13th July 1945, following a leadership ballot of the Federal Australian Labor Party. Few people had any idea how much longer the war in the Pacific would continue. And few people in the world, and probably none in Australia, knew that the United States of America had developed devastating, new weapons that would change the world forever, or that they planned to drop these weapons on the Japanese cities of Hiroshima and Nagasaki.

The dropping of atomic bombs on Hiroshima on 6th August 1945 and on Nagasaki three days later brought about the end of the Pacific war, with Emperor Hirohito announcing the Japanese surrender on 15th August 1945.

On the morning of Wednesday 15th August 1945, the Australian Prime Minister spoke on national radio to the people of Australia.

Fellow citizens, he said. *The war is over!* [1]

Chifley spoke for a further five minutes, giving thanks for the Australian sacrifices on the battlefield and at home, sentiments that were truly shared by the entire nation. Yet, right at that moment, it was those first six words that had the greatest impact and that would be remembered and celebrated long after.

Church bells rang out across the nation. In towns and cities across Australia, Chifley's broadcast, in his flat and dour voice, was heard in homes, offices, shops, factories and other workplaces. It was heard on railway platforms and in post offices. It was heard in farmhouses, barns, and shearing sheds in the countryside, and the normally phlegmatic, laconic farmers threw their hats in the air and shouted in celebration. Never before in Australian history had six words triggered such spontaneous displays of joy and celebration.

Jim White heard the broadcast at Krugers sawmill in Ipswich where the sawmill management had shut down the mill and called the men to the office veranda. A radio had been set up there, for notice had been given earlier that the Prime Minister would be making a momentous announcement. All the workmen threw their hats in the air and embraced one another when Ben Chifley spoke those long-awaited words – "The war is over!"

"The sawmill's closed for today," the mill manager shouted over the celebrations. "Go and celebrate with your families."

Jim returned to Bundamba as quickly as he could. Already the trains were starting to fill up with revellers heading into Brisbane for the main celebrations, and the streets in and around Ipswich were being covered in tickertape. At Station Road, Jim found his family, including Iris, already celebrating in the street with neighbours. All were dancing and singing — apart from Percy. Percy was there dancing and celebrating in the street along with the others, but he had found it impossible to sing with a pipe in his mouth.

"Get your dancing shoes on," Jim told his wife, "We're going to Brisbane to celebrate. Queen Street is the place to be today."

They rushed to the railway station and joined the crush of partygoers crowding onto the trains. It seemed everyone was heading to Brisbane, many of them already intoxicated — some with excitement, some with alcohol. With thousands of others in Queen Street and throughout the central business district of Brisbane, and with millions across Australia, Jim and Iris sang and danced and embraced strangers from noon on, well into the night. At last, they could celebrate as Europeans had celebrated the war in Europe, almost four months earlier. Queen Street had never seen such celebrations.

Fig. 4. Queen Street, Brisbane, 15th August 1945, two hours after Prime Minister Chifley's broadcast.

On returning to Bundamba, however, and with the resumption of their mundane lifestyle, an issue that had been eating away at Iris for some months came to the fore. Perhaps it was the emotional let-down after the euphoria of the celebrations. Perhaps it was just that she had been suppressing a troubling apprehension for too long. Or perhaps it was the long hours Jim was working, leaving her at home with her in-laws for most of the day. Whatever it was, something triggered her resolve to get the issue out in the open.

"Jim," she said, "I'm not welcome in this house."

Jim looked at his wife in astonishment. He said nothing, but the expression on his face made it quite clear he had no idea what she was talking about.

"It's your mother, Jim. She makes no pretence of even tolerating me, and I don't think I can put up with it much longer."

"You're imagining it," Jim replied. "That's just her way. Give it time. It'll work out fine."

"My parents never treated you like this," Iris protested. "You were always part of our family."

"And you're part of our family," Jim retorted, angrily, with his voice becoming louder. "You know that!"

Iris shook her head.

"No, I'm not. Your father's lovely," she said, brushing the tears from her cheeks and trying to force a smile, "apart from the smell of his pipe tobacco, that is." She paused again, then went on. "And Ruby's nice to me too, but your mother isn't going to accept me."

"That's rubbish!"

"You don't know, Jim" she said. "You're not here. You're at work all day, six days a week, and I'm left here with a woman who can't stand to have me in her house."

Jim reached out to embrace his wife, not knowing what he could say to alleviate her distress.

"She doesn't think I'm good enough for you, Jim," Iris continued, as she wept in his embrace. "I don't think anyone would be good enough for her precious Jimmy!"

"Iris, that's not true. It's probably just that she never had an opportunity to meet you before we were married. She'll come around soon."

Iris broke away from her husband's embrace, brushed the tears from her cheeks and turned to walk away, but not before issuing something of an ultimatum.

"We're moving out, Jim. Either you find a house of our own that we can rent, or I'm going back to Glen Innes."

Jim found a house to rent on Brisbane Road, Ebbw Vale, about a mile from his family home in Bundamba. The small house was very basic, and they had little in the way of furniture, cooking utensils and even crockery. Yet despite that, Iris was happy, and they lived there until early 1947. During that time, Percy was a frequent visitor, and they saw Percy, Mary and Ruby at Salvation Army meetings, but Iris very rarely visited the house at Station Road, Bundamba. Her relationship with her mother-in-law was fraught with tension and would remain so for the rest of their lives.

Financially, times were difficult for Jim and Iris. In the years after the Second World War, wages in Queensland were low, the lowest in Australia. Meeting the rent payments was a problem and this became more acute when Iris discovered she was pregnant with their first child. She wrote regularly to her family in Glen Innes and, in one letter in mid-1947, she mentioned the difficulties they faced living on Jim's small wage. She did not mention the tensions with her mother-in-law, however, nor the possibility or, in her mind, the impossibility, of moving back in with her in-laws, but perhaps her parents were astute enough to read between the lines.

The reply, when it came, was written by her father, Solomon — unusual in that letters from Glen Innes were normally written by Ella. Iris read the letter to Jim as they sat around their dinner table that night.

Wages are higher in New South Wales, everybody knows that Solomon had written. *There's a large sawmill here, the Potter & Greenway mill. You've probably seen it. I know Eric Potter and, if you would like me to, I could speak to him and enquire whether they are taking on any extra sawmill hands. Let me know if you are interested in that.*

And, Jim thought, *the unspoken message in that letter is that they'd love to have Iris back in time for the birth of our first child — their first grandchild,* but he didn't give voice to those thoughts.

"So, what do you think?" Iris asked. "Would we be better off in Glen Innes?"

Jim gave it some thought before answering. He was only too aware of the financial difficulties they were in and was resigned to the fact that there would be no reconciliation between his wife and his mother.

"Well," he eventually said, "it can't hurt for your father to make some enquiries"

"G'day, Eric," Solomon said as he entered the sawmill office.

"Sol!" Eric Potter replied, looking up from his ledger. "How are you, mate?"

"Can't complain, Eric. Can't complain."

"What can I do for you, Sol?"

"Well, Eric, my daughter and son-in-law live in Queensland and there's a possibility they might move back here to Glen Innes. The son-in-law is a sawmill worker, and I was wondering whether you might be taking on any extra hands?"

"How old is he?" Potter asked, "and which mill does he work for?"

"He must be twenty-eight or maybe twenty-nine by now," Solomon replied. "He works for Krugers Sawmill in Ipswich. You could call Krugers and ask about him if you want."

"That won't be necessary, Sol," Potter replied. "I know Krugers. He wouldn't be working for them if he wasn't a good worker. You can tell him there's a job for him at Potter and Greenway if he wants to move here."

Jim and Iris moved back to Glen Innes in September 1947 and lived for a short time with Iris's parents at the Church Street home, before renting a small cottage without electricity in Mann's Lane, on the other side of town.

1. https://anzacportal.dva.gov.au/resources/chifley-victory-speech

14
(1948 – 1965)

Moving back to Glen Innes also reconnected Iris and Jim with the extended Schoupp family. Joyce, Audrey and Maureen were still living at their parents' home.

Audrey June Schoupp would later marry Neville Wilfred Clarke on 18th October 1952 and move to the south coast of New South Wales, near Wollongong. Together they would have three daughters — Diane Fay, born 6th January 1955; Lynette Anne born 30th March 1956; and Cheryl Gay born 18th January 1960.

Maureen Margaret Schoupp would later marry Harold Ian Miller in 1960. They too would move to the area near Wollongong and together they would have one son, Garry Wayne born 4th February 1964, and one daughter, Tracy Fay, born 13th December 1970.

Mary Joyce Schoupp would later marry Leslie Victor McLachlan, a widower, on 23rd February 1974. They had no children together.

Iris's brother, Lionel Henry Schoupp, at the time of Iris and Jim's return to Glen Innes, still lived in the town, but had married Maxine Jean Elliot on 1st February 1947. Lionel and Maxine would ultimately have five children — Rodney James, born 11th April 1948; Janine Margaret, born 19th September 1949; Stephen John, born 16th January 1951; Phillip Elliott, born 24th May 1952; and Paul Richard would be born 25th September 1957.

Iris and the Schoupp family were in regular contact by letter with Iris's older sister Phyllis and her brother Dudley, both of whom were Salvation Army officers and were posted to various places throughout New South Wales and Queensland. Phyllis (see p.163) had remained unmarried.

The Woodbury name remained a very well-known name within the Salvation Army, particularly in New South Wales, and, in almost every place where Phyllis and Dudley were posted during their Salvation Army service, they found themselves running into people with the Woodbury name. Many happy hours were spent chatting and drawing family trees together to work out just how closely they were related.

It was while Dudley was stationed in Queensland at the Rockhampton Salvation Army that he came across a young woman whom he had first met at the Petersham Salvation Army Training College in 1943.

"Don't I know you?" he asked.

"You do," she replied. "I'll always remember you. You helped me when I was trying to enter the Training College in Petersham. I had way too many suitcases and you carried them for me."

Her name was Lillian May Hemmingway. Their friendship blossomed into romance and the two were wed on 18th June 1949. Their first child, Heather Margaret was born in Leeton, New South Wales on 29th September 1951. Sadly, their second child, a son, Howard Francis was born and died at Parkes in New South Wales on 24th November 1955. A third child, Denise Lillian was born in Broken Hill on 2nd January 1957.

Fig 1. Dudley Ernest Schoupp

Dudley and Lillian served as Corps Officers at Leeton, Crookwell, Broken Hill, Parkes, Gosford, Newcastle, Wynnum, Bundaberg, Campsie, Sydney Congress Hall and Brisbane City Temple. In the middle of that was a stint of five years in New Zealand, at Dunedin and Napier. In 1976, they were appointed to the position of Divisional Commanders of the North Queensland Division, and finally finished their service in the Salvation Army as Divisional Commanders of the Sydney West Division. They had given distinguished service to the Salvation Army over many years and would retire in 1990 with the rank of Lieutenant-Colonel.

Jim White took a job with the Potter & Greenway sawmill in Glen Innes, sometimes working within the mill but more often hauling large logs from the Gibraltar Range east of Glen Innes.

Fig. 3. Jim White standing at the end (not on top) of large logs being harvested from the Gibraltar Range, between Glen Innes and Grafton, c. 1948.

Life was simple in Glen Innes at that time. Wages were good, rent was very cheap on the small cottage, and Jim found he slotted easily back into Iris's extended family which now also included the family of Ella's sister and brother-in-law, the Sweeney family. These two families created a large and warm family environment which Iris and Jim were happy to be part of. Yet Jim missed his family in Bundamba, especially his younger sister, Flo, and planned to return for short visits whenever possible.

Solomon and Ella Schoupp were excited about the imminent birth of Iris and Jim's first child, for the child would also be the first-born grandchild of the Schoupp family. The child, a boy, was born in the small cottage in

Mann's Lane on 12th January 1948, with Iris's mother, Ella, acting as midwife. They named the child Ian John. For the Schoupp family, it was the commencement of a generational change — new grandchildren would be born to Iris's siblings, but at the same time the older generation was dying off.

Ella's father, Iris's grandfather, Ernest Nerney, died in Flemington, Melbourne, on 9th October 1948 whilst visiting his eldest daughter, Eveline, (known as Eva). His body was transported back to Glen Innes to be buried alongside his wife, Mary, in the Salvation Army section of the Glen Innes cemetery.

Sometime after the birth of her first child, Ian, Iris returned to working for the Wharton family. On those occasions, Ella cared for her grandson at the Church Street house. Iris and Jim were saving as much of their wages as they could, wanting to buy their own house as soon as possible. In 1950, with a little help from Iris's parents, they were able to purchase a large block of land in West Avenue, next door to the home of Olive and Hilton Sweeney, and Jim began to plan the building of their own house. Potter & Greenway were very generous and provided most of the timber free of charge and the foundations were laid in early 1952. Percy White came from Bundamba to help Jim with the building of the house and, in the early 1950s it was not unusual to find Ian, by then a toddler, sitting on the floor while Percy and Jim literally built the house around him.

By late 1952, Iris's mother, Ella, was suffering the early stages of ovarian cancer, a disease which would ultimately claim her life in 1963. Her daughter, Phyllis, resigned from her position as a Salvation Army officer and returned to Glen Innes to help care for her parents during their latter years. She took a job as receptionist for a local GP in Glen Innes but was troubled by the good doctor's questionable morals and ethics and she left that position to work as receptionist for another Glen Innes GP, Dr Victor Early. She loved working for Dr Early, whom she held in very high esteem, and she would hold that position until her death in 1973.

During the day Phyllis would go to work at the doctor's rooms and her sister, Iris, would care for their mother. At the end of the day's work, Phyllis would come home and take over the care of their mother again, while Iris returned to her own family. Phyllis was well-known, highly respected and well-loved within the Glen Innes community.

After ten years working at the Potter & Greenway sawmill in Glen Innes, Jim resigned in 1957 and took an easier job as caretaker of the Glen Innes Town Hall. It was a job that allowed his son, Ian, to walk to the Town Hall after school, and the two would spend a couple of hours together and then go home.

Jim treasured those hours spent with his son every day for the two had grown very close. Unlike other boys of his age in the neighbourhood, Ian chose to spend every available hour with his father. Rather than joining with the other boys in normal boyhood activities like building billy-carts or catching yabbies in the park creek, Ian would be with his father, tinkering with the car engine, making repairs around the house or even helping to tend the vegetable garden behind the house.

He's like my little shadow, Jim thought. And, indeed, that is what others said as well. The two were enthusiastic fishermen and, on weekends, would often escape to a riverbank to spend idyllic hours together.

They fished in many rivers, some close to town and others that meant an overnight trip to rivers west of Inverell, or east towards Grafton. One sunny Saturday afternoon, sitting on the banks of the Beardy River at Yarraford, quite close to town, Ian commented about the slow-moving, muddy water of the river.

"It's very different from the Mann River at Jackadgery, isn't it, Dad?"

Jim nodded and smiled at his son's growing awareness of nature around him. *I love these precious times I get to spend alone with my boy,* he thought.

"Every river's different, son," Jim then said. "Every river has a beauty of its own. Look at this one. See how the slow-moving water makes the river reeds sway and dance in perfect unison? It's beautiful."

"But we caught more fish at Jackadgery," Ian said.

"Yes, the Mann at Jackadgery is shallower. It babbles along over all the smooth river stones there and splashes against large rocks at times too. I always think those rocks seem to grow right out of the riverbed. The Mann's beautiful in its own way, but it's not better — just different.."

Ian sat quietly for some time after that.

"You know, son," Jim said eventually, "we tell your mum we're going fishing, but we're not. Going fishing has absolutely nothing to do with catching fish. It's about finding a place that refreshes and calms the mind and the heart."

It would be some years before Ian would come to know and appreciate what his father was talking about, but Jim continued to teach and encourage his son. Jim knew it was important to find that place that refreshes a man's spirit and nurtures that of a young boy. Others would find that place in their own way, but Jim and his son found it in the company of each other, on the riverbanks.

And, when they came home from a fishing trip, Iris would never ask, "Did you catch anything?" but rather, "Did you have a good time?", because Jim had taught her the same thing.

Ian learned the important lessons of life from his father, most of them on a riverbank somewhere.

"Let me show you something," Jim said to his son on one of those afternoons at the Town Hall. "Come with me."

They climbed the internal ladders into the upper reaches of the Town Hall, past the large clock face and higher into the bell tower where there were two huge bells with large steel hammers poised over them.

"Wow," said ten-year-old Ian. "Are these the bells we can hear from our house?"

"Yes, they are," Jim replied, "even though our house is a couple of miles from here."

Ian stared at the huge bells in wonder.

"And," Jim continued, "it's one minute to five. The bells are going to sound the hour in one minute. Get ready!"

They clamped their hands over their ears and sat there laughing while the bells rang out the hour for all of Glen Innes. When the bells fell silent, father and son went even higher, to the very top of the Town Hall, their ears still ringing, to lower the flag for the day.

A second child was born to Jim and Iris on 21st August 1959, a daughter whom they named Leanne Kaye. Leanne would later marry a local Glen Innes boy, Thomas (Tom) Anthony Manuel and together they would have two daughters, Krysten Hollee, born 5th June 1987, and Zoe Lauren, born 12th July 1992.

Late at night on 18th October 1962, there was a knock on the door of the White family home in West Avenue, Glen Innes. When Jim answered the door, he found himself standing in front of two police officers.

"Jim White?" the senior officer asked.

"Yes," Jim answered, standing there in his dressing gown.

"I'm sorry to have to inform you that your father was killed earlier this evening on Brisbane Road in Bundamba."

A car had hit and killed Percival Frederick White (Percy) whilst he was crossing the road. Percy was eighty years of age and he was buried in the Salvation Army section of Ipswich cemetery. The old man's death was a great loss to the family for it almost seemed as if Percy had been the last of a bygone pioneering era. We would not see the likes of Percy again.

The generational change continued within the Schoupp family when both Solomon and his wife, Ella, passed away in 1963. Solomon died suddenly of a stroke in Glen Innes District Hospital on 9th January 1963 at the age of seventy years. His wife, Ella, died three months later on 4th April 1963, also aged seventy, after a long illness with ovarian cancer. The two are buried side by side at the cemetery in Glen Innes.

Later that year, 1963, when the position as caretaker of the Town Hall was made redundant, Jim moved to a position with the Glen Innes Municipal Council as truck driver and as part of the road maintenance gang. It was hard, physical, work and it would ultimately take a toll on his health, perhaps even being partly the cause of an early death, but Jim was determined to provide, as best he could, for his small family.

Jim had three passions in life — his family, river fishing (usually with his son Ian), and the Glen Innes Municipal Brass Band in which he played a double base instrument for many years.

For some years, Jim tried to encourage his son to learn music and become involved in the brass band, thinking it yet another way he could spend time with his son. Yet Ian lacked the innate musical talents of his father and his grandfather, Percy. It is probably also fair to say that he lacked the necessary discipline and, to Jim's disappointment, Ian's involvement with the band was short and unremarkable.

When Ian told his father he wanted to quit the band, Jim insisted that his young son, then twelve years of age, be the one to tell the bandmaster, Eric Keating. That, too, was an important lesson in maturity — one which Jim believed important to his son's self-development.

Fig.4. Jim, on an outing with the Glen Innes Municipal Brass Band

Jim was a closet smoker which everyone knew, though he was never a heavy smoker. Iris, of course, knew Jim smoked, and Jim knew that Iris knew, but Iris disapproved to such an extent that Jim pretended he didn't smoke, and Iris pretended she didn't know.

But it was in those times alone with his son, particularly on the riverbanks, that Jim felt most at ease to roll himself a cigarette and enjoy a smoke. They would sit together on the riverbank, their fishing lines wound around Coca-Cola bottles – glass ones in those days. The Coca-Cola bottles had that gentle narrowing of diameter in the middle, rather like the waistline of a beautiful woman — just right for winding a fishing line onto, and that was one of the first things that Jim taught his son to do. They would throw their lines out into the river, using a worm or a yabby as bait, and they would push the neck of the Coca-Cola bottle into the mud. Then, they would break a twig off a tree, push it into the mud and wind the line around the top of the twig. If a fish was silly enough to take the bait, they would see the twig jerk back and forth as the fish pulled at the line. Occasionally they would pull in the line and check that the bait was still there. Occasionally, too, if it was a hot day, they would strip off and go skinny-dipping. Occasionally, they would even catch a fist. But most of the time they just talked and soaked up the peace and the beauty of the rivers.

Fig.5. Jim with his fishing line wound around a Coca-Cola bottle in one hand and, in the other, probably the best fish he ever caught in salt water.

Jim and Iris had great hopes and expectations for their son. In terms of academic success during his schooling, however, he would disappoint them. Ian attended Glen Innes Public School and then Glen Innes High School, but he was mostly a troublesome student and learned very little. Conversely, his younger sister, Leanne, when she came along, quite enjoyed attending the same schools and excelled academically. Obviously, it was not the genes.

Ian had precious little interest in school and Jim may have exacerbated that somewhat when Ian came home from his first day in high school

"I've been put in a French class," he told his father with some excitement. It was, in fact, the first school subject that had ever interested him and, sixty years on he would still remember the little French he learned that day.

Jim banged his fist on the dining table.

"We'll see about that!" he said. "We'll get you out of that useless subject!"

The next morning, Jim was at the school banging his fist on the school principal's desk. He demanded his son be taken out of the French class and placed in a woodwork class which, along with most of his other subjects, Ian dutifully failed. Ironically, in later life, after his father's death, Ian would find his forte and his life's work in the field of foreign languages.

At the end of the 1963 school year, when Ian was fifteen years of age and had just completed, after a fashion, his third year of High School, Jim was called to go and see the school principal, Frank Moroney. Old Frank was a sad case, known to have something of a drinking problem but, on this morning, he delivered his message to Jim quite clearly.

"He's wasting his time here, Mr White," Frank said. "In fact, he's wasting *our* time. I don't know how many occasions he's been sent to my office. I've had to cane him numerous times, but we've been unable to modify his behaviour."

"Perhaps part of the blame rests with the teachers," Jim replied, not wanting to acknowledge any fault in his son.

"I won't hear anything said against my staff," Frank Moroney replied. "They have to maintain order and good behaviour in the classroom, and I support them."

He picked up a copy of Ian's end of year report and read from the comments written by Ian's teachers.

"Take this one, for example," he said. "Ian's mathematics teacher, Mr Bernie Donoghue, has written, 'Ian will find it increasingly difficult to learn very much from out in the corridor.' I ask you, what are we supposed to do with him?"

Jim knew Bernie Donoghue quite well and respected him — Bernie sang in the town choir with Iris. Jim nodded, shook hands with the principal, took the report and went home to speak with his son.

"Son," he said. "I think you'd better get a job."

15
(1965 – 2020)

Ian took a retail job in one of the two large department stores in Glen Innes, Kwong Sing & Co, but was really just filling in time. His ambition was to join the Royal Australian Air Force, but he was only fifteen years of age and the minimum age requirement for the RAAF was seventeen. He sent in his application on his seventeenth birthday.

It was on an evening some months later when Ian was at a church youth-group meeting that Jim answered a knock on the door and opened it to find two police officers standing there.

"Mr Jim White?" one of them asked.

"That's right," Jim replied.

"Apparently your son has applied to join the Air Force. We've been asked to submit a security check on him," the officer said, "but we don't know him. We know most of the young lads in town, but we don't know your son."

Jim broke into a broad smile.

"Well, the fact you don't know him is the best news I've had for quite a while," he said.

Ian joined the RAAF in May 1965 and was sent for ten weeks of recruit training at RAAF Base Edinburgh, South Australia. As the platoon of recruits alighted from the bus, a screaming Corporal whom they would all soon come to hate met them and straight away verbally assaulted them.

Corporal Andy Richardson who would be their drill NCO for those ten weeks looked over the group, shaking his head in disdain. Only prudence stopped the recruits from telling him the feeling was mutual.

"Where d' y' think y' are, laddie?" he screamed at one of the recruits in his broad Scottish accent. "Y' look like y're in a brothel. Ya dinna eva put yer 'ands in yer pockets."

The recruits learned immediately that military men do not put their hands in their pockets, but just how having one's hands in one's pockets was associated with being in a brothel escaped everyone except Corporal Richardson.

"The bus 'll deliver yer luggage to yer barracks," he continued. "We're going t' the barber's shop."

He pointed in a certain direction, and the recruits began walking that way, only to be screamed at again.

"Y' dinna eva walk like a rabble 'ere!" he screamed. "'Ere, y' march…..left, right, left right."

After ten weeks of being screamed at by the sadistic Corporal Richardson, the recruits left Edinburgh and were distributed to their respective training facilities. Ian was sent to RAAF Radio School at Laverton, Victoria, where he was trained in morse code. From 1967–1969, he served at RAAF Butterworth, Malaysia and it was during that time that the RAAF first noticed Ian's aptitude for foreign languages. On his return to Australia, he was sent to RAAF School of Languages at Point Cook, Victoria, to learn Asian languages. From that time forward, Ian worked in military intelligence as a linguist/translator. During those years Ian also enrolled in night school, completing his Year 12 matriculation, followed by a tertiary degree and a Diploma of Secondary Teaching.

Phyllis Schoupp died of breast cancer in the Glen Innes District Hospital on 19th May 1973 and was buried in the Salvation Army section of the Glen Inness cemetery alongside her beloved parents. Her brother Dudley Schoupp delivered the eulogy at her funeral service.

"We have been blessed to have had a lot of fine Christian people in our family," Dudley said, "but, if there was a saint amongst them, it was undoubtedly my sister Phyllis, greatly loved by all in the family and by all who knew her."

When Ian left the RAAF in 1977, he spent the next twenty-five years teaching languages in Australian secondary schools where he held positions as Head of Language Departments in Western Australia and in Victoria. During that time, he authored more than twenty textbooks for the teaching of languages in secondary schools. Had Jim lived longer, he would undoubtedly have been proud of his son's achievements and may even have modified his earlier opinion that language study was a waste of time, and a "useless subject". Sadly, however, Jim was not to live long enough to see his son's achievements.

On 28th October 1975, James Edward White wrote a letter and mailed it to his son who at that time was serving with the Royal Australian Air Force at Pearce Air Force Base, Western Australia. For some time, Jim had been suffering from severe chest pains, unbeknown to his son and, although it had been previously diagnosed by a Sydney cardiologist as being "only muscular pain of no real concern", Jim continued to worry — and increasingly so as the pain started to become more intense. His local doctor, Dr Victor Early, believed the pain was caused by blocked arteries to the heart, so decided to refer Jim to a second cardiac specialist in Sydney. Arrangements were made for Jim to fly to Sydney, but the day prior to his planned departure, the air traffic controllers in New South Wales went on strike, grounding all aircraft. Instead of the planned flight, Jim travelled to Sydney by train. He suffered a massive heart attack during the trip, was taken off the train at Strathfield station and rushed to Old Sydney Hospital. He died in that hospital without any family by his bed, on the night of 1st November 1975.

The news of his father's death came as a great shock to his son, Ian, who rushed back to Glen Innes to be with his mother and sister as soon as the news reached him. James Edward White was buried in the Salvation Army section of the Glen Innes cemetery. He was only fifty-seven years of age.

The letter his father had written to Ian was waiting for him when he returned to RAAF Pearce several weeks later. It was the last letter Jim had ever written. It is clear from that letter that he knew how serious the problem was and that he was very worried about it.

> *I cannot walk more than a hundred yards without severe pain and can do practically nothing that causes exertion,* Jim had written. *If I must have this operation, it is not much to look forward to ......I guess I would feel better off on a fishing trip somewhere.*

Jim's wife, Stella Iris Joan White née Schoupp, outlived Jim by forty-four years, passing away in a Glen Innes nursing home on 17th August 2019 at the age of ninety-seven. In her final years, Iris suffered greatly from cancer. Her son, Ian, delivered the eulogy at her funeral service.

"Iris was ninety-seven years of age when the Lord called her home. She didn't quite live long enough to get her telegram from the Queen, but that's okay — she knew The King, and she is with him now."

Iris was buried alongside her husband, Jim, in the Salvation Army section of the Glen Innes cemetery.

Only one of the seven children born to Solomon James Schoupp and Margaret Ella Schoupp (Ella) remains alive at the time of writing. Audrey June Clarke née Schoupp lives in a nursing home, close to her daughters in the Newcastle area of New South Wales. At the time of writing, Audrey is eighty-nine years of age.

Florence (Flo) McLaren née White, Jim's younger sister, died in Buderim, Queensland (Sunshine Coast) on 7th April 2012. She was greatly loved and very much missed by the entire extended family. Her husband, and Jim's life-long friend, Wallace Dudley James McLaren (Wal), died in Buderim, Queensland, on 20th March 2014, aged 97.

Ian John White is the only son of James Edward White who, in turn, was the only son of Percival Frederick White. Percival Frederick White was the only son of Percival Pearce White (II) apart from James John White who died at five years of age. At the time of writing Ian is the only surviving member of this family who still has the surname White. Ian has never married and has no children. As the only son of an only son of an only son, the family name will die with him, a fact which causes him considerable anguish and pain. Yet he finds some solace in the fact that there are many others who are descended from this branch of the Woodbury family.

Sarah Elizabeth Woodbury née Everingham and Richard Woodbury (I) had eleven children. Those eleven descendants of Richard Woodbury (I) had a total of seventy-four children, and the number of descendants multiplied exponentially with each generation. This book has traced only the family descended from Sarah Woodbury and Richard Woodbury's youngest son, George James Woodbury, and thence through his daughter, Aquilla Woodbury. As we have seen, Aquilla married George Henry Schoupp and thus, in this branch of the family, the name Woodbury became Schoupp (see p.xii). Many members of this branch of the family still carry the name Schoupp. Denise Lillian Schoupp, daughter of Dudley Ernest Schoupp and Lillian May Schoupp, still lives in Sydney, and the four sons of Lionel Henry Schoupp (see p.203) are still alive and have themselves left numerous sons to carry forward the Schoupp name. And subsequent marriages of Aquilla's female descendants have resulted in numerous other name changes – White, Clarke, Miller, Clulow, Prince, Benson, Jier, Cadorin, Manuel, Clifton, Marchant, Piccirillo, Schiels, Hawke, Fenech.

Yet they all have one thing in common — all are part of The Woodbury Line.

AUTHOR'S CLOSING COMMENTS

Perhaps you, the reader, are trying to understand, in your own mind, which parts of this book are factual, and which are fictional. Many of the conversations, particularly those which pre-date living memory, are fictitious for they were not recorded for us. They arise from the author's desire to place family members within known facts about their lives and to produce a narrative that attempts to describe what they would likely have been thinking and what they would likely have said at those times. Some more recent conversations are as remembered by the author, or as conveyed to him by parents, grandparents, etc. The exact wording of those conversation may not be totally accurate, but they are presented honestly within the constraints of memory fallibility.

Let me try and assist you with some of the other issues covered in this book.

Charlie Doyle and his younger brother, Adam, mentioned in Chapter 6, did not exist. Charlie was created merely as a character with whom John Woodbury (b. 1854) could engage in conversation for the purpose of conveying factual background information about the Woodbury family.

The name of the WWI AIF recruiting officer in Glen Innes, Lieutenant Watson (p.123), is fictitious, though this officer did exist. I remember my grandfather, Solomon, telling me of this conversation. Even though I was a young teenager at the time, it was important to him that I understood the basis on which he had gone to war and his belief, as he impressed upon me numerous times, that "war is folly". I do not remember him mentioning the recruiting officer's name and, in fact, he might not have known the name. As was the case with many war veterans, Grandfather talked very little about the war. Indeed, the only other person from the war that Grandfather talked about was his good friend, Tommy McArdle from Tingha, who fell at Villers-Bretonneux, France, in 1918 (pp. 128 & 140).

The incident of Mary White's neighbour calling to her from the footpath in front of their home in Station Road, Bundamba (Chapter 11) is factual, although the neighbour's name has long been forgotten. Thus, the name Marcie Henderson is fictitious, though the person and the incident are not.

Stories of the decks that were built for the women of the Woodbury family's early generations persist in our family. Those stories, it must be said, are anecdotal. I have no documentary or photographic evidence that the building of such decks was a family practice, but it seems, from family lore, that it may well have been so.

The attack by three murderous escaped convicts on the Woodbury family in Gunderman in 1828 is factual, and the report quoted verbatim from the *Sydney Gazette & New South Wales Advertiser* is mostly accurate.

Reference to indigenous Australians being relegated to the status of township fringe-dwellers, sadly, is a matter of public knowledge throughout the townships of New South Wales and indeed throughout Australia. Details of the Myall Creek massacre are given accurately, including details of the seven members of the gang who were publicly hanged at Sydney Goal on 18th December 1838 for their part in that heinous crime.

All families mentioned in the book did, or do, exist, including the Nerney, Wharton, Sweeney, Hunt and

McLaren families. Potter & Greenway Sawmill in Glen Innes did exist but was closed in the late 1980s. Krugers Sawmill did exist in Ipswich and still does, though its operations are now based in Grafton, NSW.

Solomon Schoupp's dilemma about enlistment in the AIF for WWI service and his subsequent service on the Western Front as a stretcher-bearer is as he described it to this author. Details of the 33rd Battalion's actions on the Western Front are accurate. So too are the details of James Edward White's WWII service at Milne Bay and on the Kokoda Track.

The letter received from the War Office when Ella Schoupp enquired about media reports of her husband's death is accurately quoted and is part of the digitised WWI military records which can be accessed through the website of the National Archives of Australia (www.naa.gov.au). A copy of that letter is held by this author. Jim White's final letter to his son, Ian, is quoted accurately and remains in the private collection of the author.

Quotes from letters between Solomon and Ella during WWI, between Ella and her mother-in-law, Aquilla, and between Solomon and his mother, Aquilla, are fictitious, although I believe letters expressing such sentiments were almost certainly written.

Christianity has been a significant and enduring feature in the lives of the Woodbury and Schoupp families from the earliest colonial times until the present day. For the Woodbury family, that religious affiliation morphed from Church of England, through Wesleyan Methodism and ultimately to Salvation Army. For the Schoupp family, it originated in Lutheranism, then changed to Salvation Army after their arrival in Australia. It was within the Salvation Army that the two families came together in the marriage of Phillip Henry Schoupp and Aquilla Woodbury in July 1879.

Significant mention has been made of the involvement of the Woodbury and Schoupp families in the Salvation Army in Inverell, Tingha, and Glen Innes. All of it is accurate.

Articles and reports from a number of newspapers have been quoted;
The Sydney Gazette & New South Wales Advertiser
The Armidale Express & New England General Advertiser
The Brisbane Courier
The Glen Innes Examiner
The Inverell Times
The Worker (Queensland)
The Daily Mercury (Mackay, Queensland).

All are quoted accurately, and sources are cited.

Ian J White

APPENDIX I

The following pages show the children and the grandchildren of Richard Woodbury (I) and Sarah Elizabeth (Sally) Woodbury née Everingham. Those grandchildren of Richard Woodbury (I) and Sarah Elizabeth (Sally) Woodbury née Everingham, of course, would be the great-grandchildren of Matthew James Everingham and Elizabeth Everingham née Rymes.

Readers wishing to further explore these branches of the Woodbury family are directed to Valerie Ross's excellent and exhaustive genealogy, *Cornstalks 1988 – A Genealogy*, Valross Pty Limited, Sydney, 1987.

WOODBURY

Richard Woodbury (II) was the son of Richard Woodbury (I) and Sarah Elizabeth (Sally) Woodbury née Everingham, and the grandson of Matthew James Everingham and Elizabeth Everingham née Rymes. The children of Richard Woodbury (II) & Jane Woodbury née Neal were the great-grandchildren of Matthew James Everingham and Elizabeth Everingham née Rymes

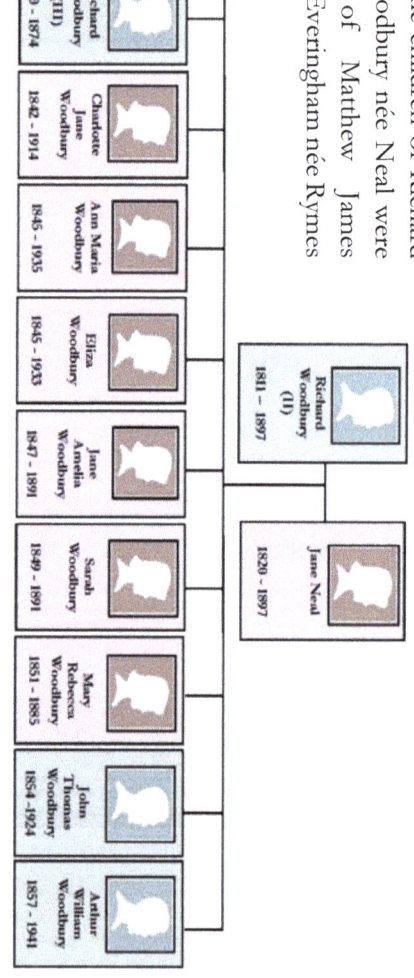

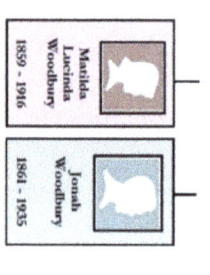

WOODBURY – HIBBS

Elizabeth Woodbury was the daughter of Richard Woodbury (I) and Sarah Elizabeth (Sally) Woodbury née Everingham. The children of Elizabeth & William Hibbs were the grandchildren of Richard Woodbury (I) and Sarah Elizabeth (Sally) Woodbury née Everingham and the great-grandchildren of Matthew James Everingham and Elizabeth Everingham née Rymes.

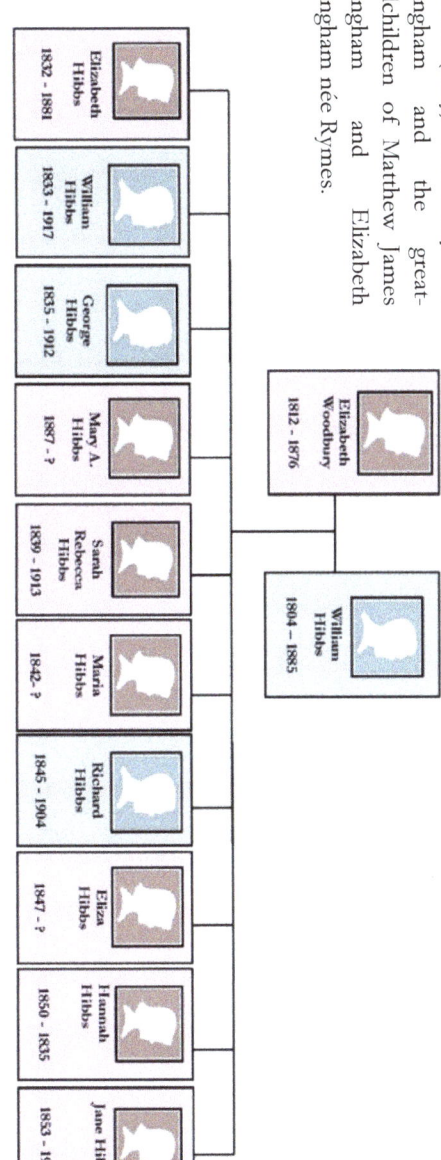

WOODBURY

William Woodbury (I) was the son of Richard Woodbury (I) and Sarah Elizabeth (Sally) Woodbury née Everingham. The children of Elizabeth & William Hibbs were the grandchildren of Richard Woodbury (I) and Sarah Elizabeth (Sally) Woodbury née Everingham and the great-grandchildren of Matthew James Everingham & Elizabeth Everingham née Rymes.

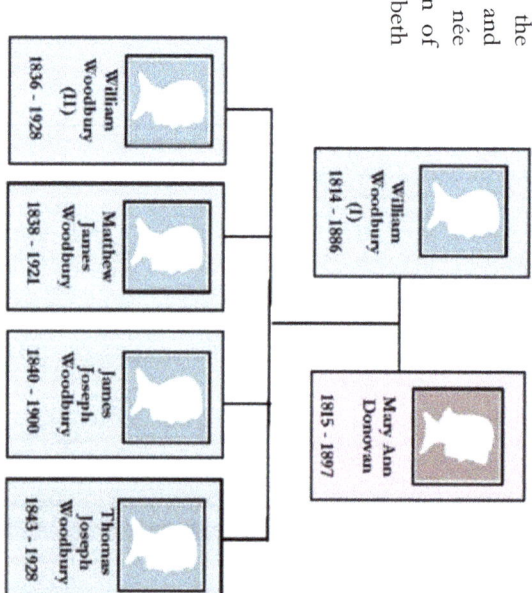

WOODBURY

Jeremiah Woodbury (I) was the son of Richard Woodbury (I) and Sarah Elizabeth (Sally) Woodbury née Everingham. The children of Jeremiah Woodbury (I) & Maria Woodbury née Chaseling were the great-grandchildren of Matthew James Everingham & Elizabeth Everingham née Rymes.

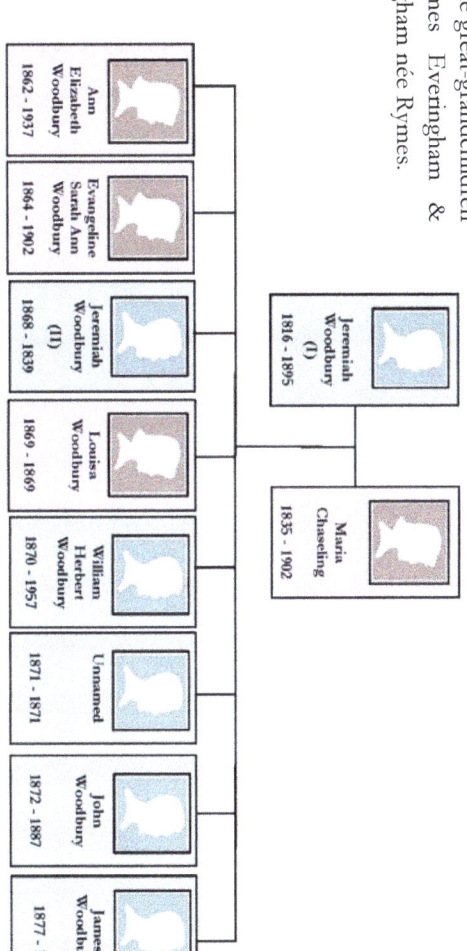

WOODBURY - BRIDGE

Sarah Woodbury (II) was the daughter of Richard Woodbury (I) and Sarah Elizabeth (Sally) Woodbury née Everingham. The children of Sarah & Joseph Bridge were the great-grandchildren of Matthew James Everingham & Elizabeth Everingham née Rymes.

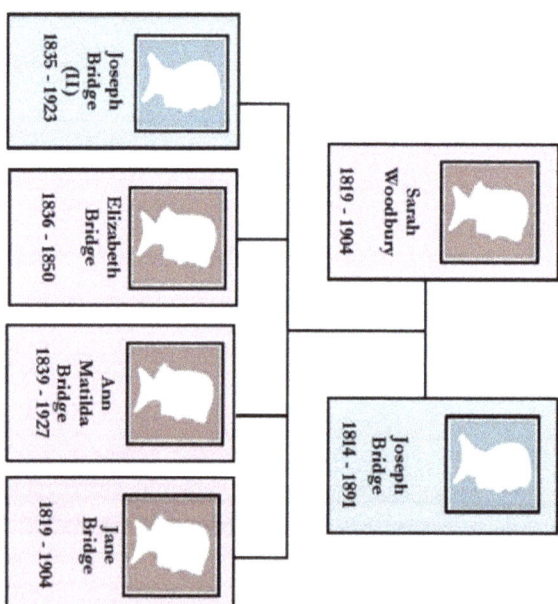

WOODBURY - CRAFT

Rebecca Woodbury was the daughter of Richard Woodbury (I) and Sarah Elizabeth (Sally) Woodbury née Everingham. The children of Rebecca & William Craft were the great-grandchildren of Matthew James Everingham & Elizabeth Everingham née Rymes.

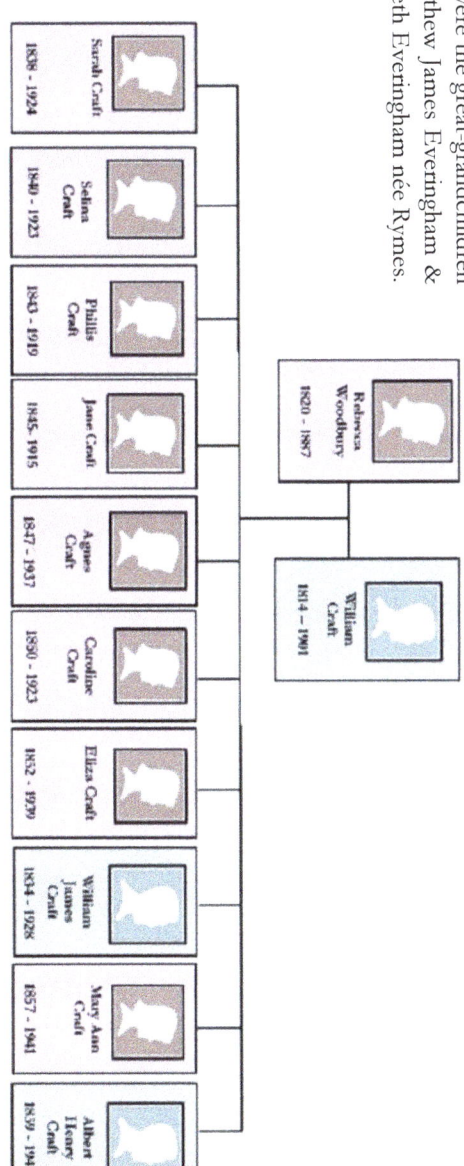

WOODBURY

John Woodbury was the son of Richard Woodbury (I) and Sarah Elizabeth (Sally) Woodbury née Everingham. The children of John & Mary Woodbury were were the great-grandchildren of Matthew James Everingham & Elizabeth Everingham née Rymes.

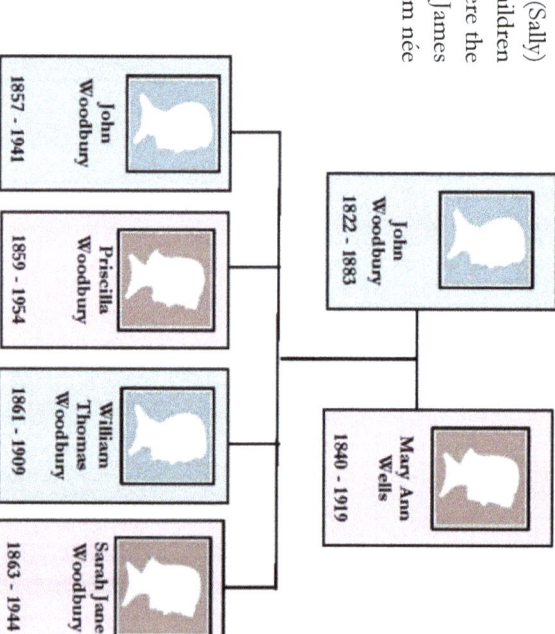

WOODBURY – CRAFT - DOVEY

Anne Woodbury was the daughter of Richard Woodbury (I) and Sarah Elizabeth (Sally) Woodbury née Everingham. Ann Woodbury married first James Craft (July 1840) and second Adam Dovey (Feb. 1858) after the death of James Craft. The children of Ann & James Craft were the great-grandchildren of Matthew James Everingham & Elizabeth Everingham née Rymes.

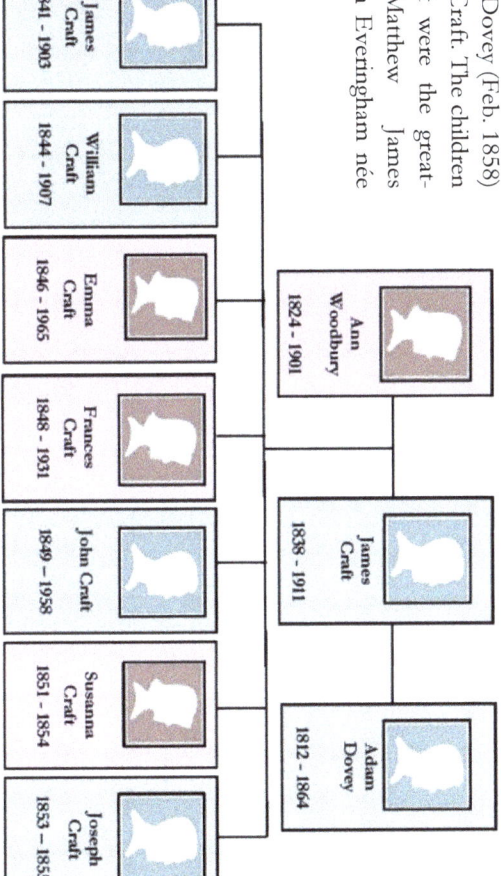

WOODBURY – CORNWELL

Jane Woodbury was the daughter of Richard Woodbury (I) and Sarah Elizabeth (Sally) Woodbury née Everingham. The children of Jane Cornell née Woodbury & John P. Cornwell (I) were the great-grandchildren of Matthew James Everingham & Elizabeth Everingham née Rymes.

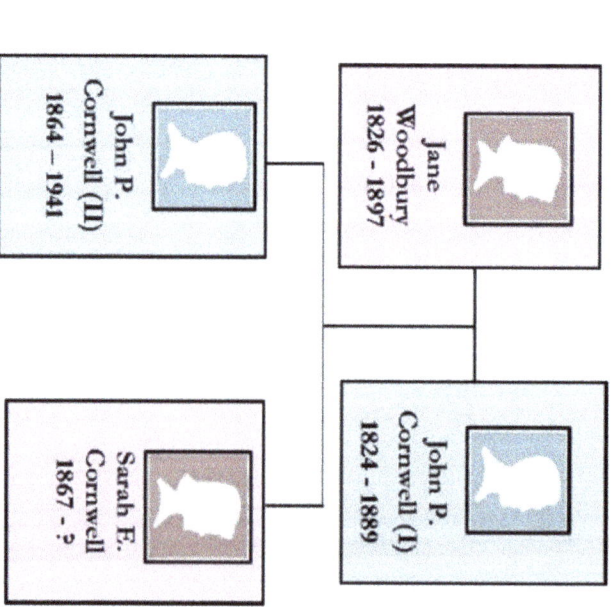

WOODBURY

Matthew James Woodbury was the son of Richard Woodbury (I) and Sarah Elizabeth (Sally) Woodbury née Everingham. He was born 15th July 1828 in Windsor, NSW, and died at the age of seven years on 23rd November 1835 in Laughtondale, NSW. Having died at the age of seven years, of course, he did not marry and had no children

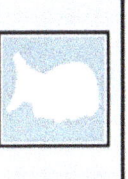

Matthew James Woodbury
1828 - 1835

WOODBURY

George James Woodbury was the youngest child of Richard Woodbury (I) and Sarah Elizabeth (Sally) Woodbury née Everingham. The children of George James Woodbury & Sarah Elizabeth Pate Woodbury née Charter were the great-grandchildren of Matthew James Everingham & Elizabeth Everingham née Rymes.

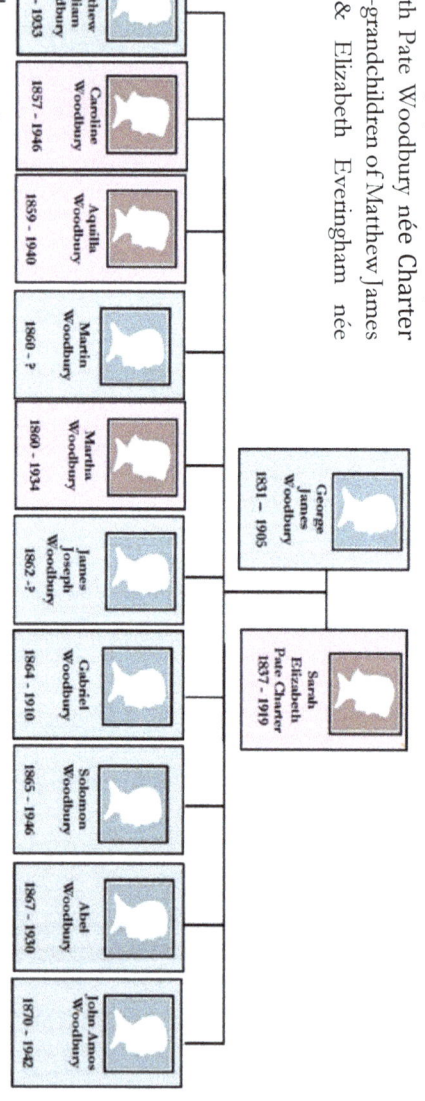

OTHER BOOKS BY THIS AUTHOR

Brand New Every Morning
A daily guide to reading the Bible in one year

The Mustard Seed
God's plan for New Creation

Glass Half Full
An uplifting book of encouragement for Christians and for non-Christians alike as we attempt to deal with the rollercoaster ride of life

Elizabeth Rymes – A Remarkable Life
The life and times of Elizabeth Rymes, a truly remarkable woman pioneer in the early colonial days of Australia

Details of all books can be found at
www.themustardseed.net.au/books

Coming Soon

Matthew James Everingham – Convict of the First Fleet

www.ingramcontent.com/pod-product-compliance
Lightning Source LLC
Chambersburg PA
CBHW051535010526
44107CB00064B/2737